HIDD
NORF

Keith Skipper

COUNTRYSIDE BOOKS
NEWBURY • BERKSHIRE

First published 1998
© Keith Skipper 1998

COUNTRYSIDE BOOKS
3 Catherine Road
Newbury, Berkshire

ISBN 1 85306 515 3

*Dedicated to my wife Diane and
our sons Danny and Robin –
constant companions on travels round
my beloved Norfolk.*

Illustrations and map by Jason Partner

The front cover photograph taken by Rod Edwards
shows the windmill and reedbeds at Cley-next-the-Sea.

The back cover photograph taken by the author
shows the wall of the Old Post Office at Plumstead,
with its painting of a Penny Black stamp.

Produced through MRM Associates Ltd., Reading
Printed by J. W. Arrowsmith Ltd., Bristol

INTRODUCTION

Just when I thought it was safe to claim a comprehensive knowledge of my native county . . .

Well, the invitation to go in search of Norfolk's quieter corners and some of its lesser-lauded personalities proved a rather humbling experience. Several times I got the feeling that I was simply scratching the surface with thumbnail sketches and flying visits.

Yes, I renewed acquaintance with several old friends, but some of them have changed almost beyond recognition since our previous meetings – and there's no doubt that I looked a bit different from the lad who biked towards so many wonderful discoveries over 40 years ago.

No, Norfolk has not completely surrendered its precious character to hordes of speculators and spoilers, but there are enough ominous signs to alert locals and visitors alike to possible dangers ahead. Not so easy to bike in comfort for a start.

Family and friends put up with my many moods as I probed, inspected, collated, wandered, scribbled and sought enlightenment from friendly natives. My wife, Diane, was a constant source of support, not just in her driving duties on countless expeditions but also with her technological wizardry when it came to sorting it all out for publication.

I am also grateful to my old friend Jason Partner, one of the region's top water-colour artists and an eagerly-adopted son of Norfolk, for his outstanding illustrations. He renewed my appetite for the familiar by presenting it in an entirely new light.

My thanks, too, to Nicholas Battle and Countryside Books for the opportunities to remind myself of Norfolk's unfading delights at a time when it is sheer folly to take them for granted.

Keith Skipper
Cromer, Norfolk

ACLE

It has been claimed many times that Norfolk has avoided the over-developed fate of other counties by virtue of being 'on the road to nowhere'. Certainly, geography has bequeathed an isolation to shape character and help protect it. What is not commonly known is that Norfolk really does have a road to Nowhere, a road that goes back to the 11th century.

Under the provision of the Assessment Act of 1862, Nowhere was annexed to the parish of Acle, pronounced Aycull (say it quickly), a gateway to the Norfolk Broads positioned roughly between Norwich and Great Yarmouth. In the 11th century many villages had salt pans, that is salt marshes flooded by high tides. They were dammed off and the sun dried the marsh. This left a residue of salt, collected and used to preserve fish and foodstuffs. Surrounding parishes therefore had isolated marshes miles from their boundaries. Miles from anywhere – Nowhere, in fact! That's how the name emerged.

The Norfolk Archaeological Unit excavated a site – about a mile from Yarmouth beside the river Bure to the north of the Acle Straight road – in the 1940s and found medieval pottery, firmly suggesting it was the home of the local salt pans. This is part of Nowhere, although the name was changed in the early 20th century to White House Farm.

Evidently, it was altered after a Mr Bailey had trouble with the law. He had been to Yarmouth to sell some cattle and celebrated quite liberally after a successful day. A local policeman had cause to speak to him and asked where he lived. Mr Bailey's reply of 'Nowhere' was construed as being less than helpful – the constable was not too familiar with the area – and this led to a decision to change the address. White House Farm sounded a much more likely destination for a farmer giving vent to his cheerful feelings after a lucrative day in town.

Mind you, that doesn't stop some of today's puckish locals having a bit of fun with newcomers and holidaymakers. Jokes about 'going Nowhere' should be taken with a big pinch of salt.

There are several other claimants for a Nowhere location in Norfolk, including Great Witchingham, Wiveton and Wereham.

For me, however, the Acle connection is the best documented and most convincing.

 ## ALDBOROUGH

—— Often confused with Aldeburgh, the Suffolk coastal town made famous in international circles through the festival of music established by Benjamin Britten, this Norfolk village a few miles inland from Cromer strikes more homely notes. It clusters round the green, a natural recreation centre edged with history.

King John granted the charter for a fair on the green in June each year, originally for the sale of horses, livestock, poultry and household goods as well as for hiring servants and labourers. Late last century it turned into more of a pleasure fair and that is the general format today.

For cricket enthusiasts, players, umpires and spectators alike, this is one of the favourite settings in the area. They have played here for over 150 years with about 30 cottages surrounding the pitch like eager fieldsmen. There's a Long Stop Cottage, First Slip Cottage and Second Slip Cottage. There was a time when the village team was made up of those who lived just beyond the boundary. When the parson, the doctor and the blacksmith were on parade the occasional broken window was viewed indulgently. Now, with some of the houses renovated and used as holiday cottages, such antics can draw sharp complaints.

It was June but pouring with rain when I called to renew acquaintance with a sporting arena I first played on over 30 years ago. Neither the weather nor the fact I scored no runs and took no wickets on my initial appearance against Aldborough could dim the pleasure of memories fashioned out of one of Norfolk's most idyllic village scenes.

ALDERFORD COMMON

—— This haven for wildlife, nightingales in particular, straddles the Norwich to Reepham road eight miles north-west of the city. The common, covering about 35 acres, lies in the south-west corner of the parish of Swannington and has been a Site of Special Scientific Interest since 1957. An overgrown Bronze Age round barrow suggests this land may never have been ploughed. Traditional grazing, carried on since the Middle Ages with cattle, goats and chickens, petered out during the 1960s. An old lime kiln has become an important hibernation site for bats as well as a backcloth for countless 'Famous Five' adventures starring brave local youngsters. A large part of the common was the scene of intensive digging of chalk and marl and this has led to a big increase in the wildlife interest of the site. The marlpit area is one of the best examples of chalk grassland in Norfolk, with a wide range of uncommon wild flowers. The rest of the common is made up of open areas, now covered with bracken, hawthorn and blackthorn scrub, and plenty of trees, mainly ash, birch and oak. These provide roosting sites in winter for many hundreds of thrushes. The scrub also serves up good nesting sites for a wide range of birds including willow warbler, chiffchaff, blackcap, whitethroat, lesser whitethroat and especially nightingales.

The National Nightingale Survey of 1980 showed there were more pairs of nightingales holding territories on Alderford Common than on any other site in east Norfolk.

ANTINGHAM

It may be a pity to let boring old facts and theories get in the way of a lovely legend. But, sadly, there is no clear evidence to support the story that the two churches in one churchyard at Antingham were built by two sisters after whom they were named. St Margaret's has been in ruins since the beginning of the 18th century. Only the tower and part of the nave remain, smothered in ivy. A bright, welcoming church, St Mary's lives on next door and since 1965 has been part of the Trunch Team Ministry of Ten, one of the first such groupings to be established in this country. By the end of the 17th century Antingham had decided it could no longer support two churches and St Margaret's was abandoned. After 1701 the living of St Margaret's passed to the Vicar of North Walsham, whose successors have continued to hold it in plurality. The ruin is the responsibility of the Parochial Church Council of North Walsham rather than Antingham. There is evidence of at least twelve examples of the Antingham situation in Norfolk in the Middle Ages.

The reason for the two churches here may have something to do with divided lordship of manorial land or with the competing claims of English and Danish inhabitants. St Margaret's shows evidence of 12th-century work while St Mary's dates from about 1330. The whole church was probably built within a period of 30 years from that date as the windows are almost exclusively in the decorated style of three lights with reticulated tracery. There is also no structural division between the nave and the chancel and the tower is clearly of a date with the rest of the church. Only the font belongs to an earlier period, possibly not later than 1225, and it seems reasonable to suppose it once belonged to St Margaret's.

The phenomenon of two churches in the same graveyard is repeated at Great Melton and South Walsham. The highest concentration of all was at Reepham which had, until the 16th century, three functioning churches in one yard.

ARMINGHALL

——— A monument built between four and five thousand years ago was discovered here, just south of Norwich, by a pioneer of archaeological air photography.

Wing Commander Insall made his flight in 1929 to reveal the Arminghall henge, described by David Dymond in his book *The Norfolk Landscape* (published 1985) as 'the most powerful symbol yet found in Norfolk of Neolithic man's increasing control of his environment, as well as of his social organisation and religious beliefs'.

A large circular bank 50 feet wide, with external and internal ditches, surrounded a central space with a diameter of 90 feet. Here a horseshoe of eight large holes once contained huge timber posts up to three feet in diameter and sunk into the ground to a depth of seven and a half feet. It is not known whether the posts were free-standing 'totems' or supported a roofed building. Either way, this technological and symbolic achievement is as impressive for its time as the building, 3,000 years later and only a couple of miles away in the next valley, of Norwich Cathedral.

The site is now a scheduled ancient monument and lies under pasture. It is accessible from a public footpath which runs past its northern edge from White Horse Lane in the east to the Lakenham-Caistor St Edmund road in the west.

ASHILL

The population has trebled to over 1,500 during the past three decades in this village between Swaffham and Watton. That's in direct contrast to the unhurried and largely unchanged scene of the 19th century personified by the faithful Bartholomew Edwards. He died just nine days short of his one hundredth birthday and was Rector of Ashill for 76 years, one of the longest incumbencies on record.

He never retired, never went away for a holiday and hardly missed a service. Father of the Ashill flock from 1813 until his death in 1889, he buried village folk he had baptised as children.

He built the vestry in the parish church of St Nicholas, some parts of which are 700 years old, and there are memorial slates to him and his wife on the north side. The east window was restored in 1806 and filled with painted glass. This was replaced by the present stained glass in 1900 in memory of the long-serving Rev. Bartholomew Edwards.

While Ashill may not have altered much during his time, the village did develop a radical reputation when it came to open protest over the loss of ancient common land. An anonymous letter sent to a local newspaper in 1816 accused local farmers of greedy exploitation and threatened them with violence and death: 'You do as you like, you rob the poor of their common right, plough the grass up that God sent to grow . . . and lay muck and stones on the road to prevent grass growing.' Today the goose green and village pond are in the charge of the village trustees, who also administer charitable funds.

This expanding Norfolk town grew up on the main road from Norwich to London. Few travellers in this age of the car trouble to stop and explore. Speeding by on the bypass is the general rule today. I urge you to slow down and take in at least three of Attleborough's impressive salutes to the past.

In 1675 what may well have been the first of the turnpike roads was built between Attleborough and Wymondham. A gift of £200 was given by the aptly-named Sir Edward Riches for the repair and upkeep of the road. His generosity was marked by a square stone pillar located on the Norwich side of the old A11 trunk road. The pillar was renovated in 1888 and inscribed: 'This pillar was erected by the order of the session of the Peace of Norfolk as a grateful rememberance of the charity of Sir Edwin Rich, Kt, who freely gave ye sume of Two Hundred pounds towards ye repair of ye highway between Wymondham and Attleburgh, A.D. 1675'. Edwin Rich mentioned on the pillar is taken to be the Edward Riches named in contemporary documents.

In the town itself a monument stands at the junction of Station Road and Connaught Road, dedicated to the battles of the Crimean War (1854–1856). It is rare to find in any town a monument dedicated to this war. Standing well over 15 feet tall, it has been restored several times and survived being hit in 1983 by a passing car. The monument bears on its four sides the names of famous battles associated with the Crimea – Balaclava, Inkerman, Alma and Sebastopol, together with the inscription 'Peace 1856'.

The acorn-crowned water pump of Queen's Square was erected to celebrate Queen Victoria's jubilee in 1897. At one time, before the blessing of piped water, it would have been vital to the community. It is a tree pump, carved from a single tree trunk that has been bored through and clamped around with iron brackets. The pump hasn't been used since the 1930s. Older residents used to claim that water from this pump was much purer than any other.

On entering the ever-bustling market place of this attractive Norfolk town, it is easy to miss a salute to the only militant Jacobite the county ever produced. The tablet on the wall of Barclay's Bank reads: 'Christopher Layer of Booton lived here. He was a faithful adherent of the House of Stuart and for his loyalty to that cause suffered an ignominious death at Tyburn, 17th May, 1723.'

The tribute was set up by Prince Frederick Duleep Singh in 1908. Himself a member of a ruling family exiled for generations from their own domains, Prince Frederick developed a warm and romantic attachment to the Stuart line, and magnified Layer's rather ineffective efforts into heroic adventures.

Layer was a broken-down lawyer who sought to acquire fame and fortune by helping bring about the return of the exiled house. Most of his projects were absurd, but he displayed admirable fortitude throughout his imprisonment and trial, refusing to give away any secrets or to incriminate any associates. Layer had drifted into the tangled web of Jacobite conspiracy, visiting the Pretender in Italy and then meeting leading agents in France. On his return he became closely associated with the main Jacobites and gave in to a mood of reckless daring. It was said afterwards that he expected to become Lord Chancellor under the new regime and was quite prepared to take risks in pursuit of that prize. Layer was arrested and after prolonged examination was sent to the Tower in September 1722. He went on trial for high treason two months later. His execution was postponed seven times. On the gallows he behaved calmly and with courage, making a brief speech to the effect the nation would never be happy and prosperous until it was once more under the rule of its rightful King. Layer's head was fixed on a post above Temple Bar as a warning to others.

See Blo Norton entry for more on Prince Frederick Duleep Singh.

This small nook of the Royal Estate around Sandringham is notable for two churches, ancient and modern, left to find solace in yesterday's songs of praise.

Across the fields St Felix beckons to his old headquarters, ruined and lonely, draped with ivy but still tinged with pride at being lauded as the site of the first Christian church in East Anglia. St Felix had followed St Augustine early in the 7th century and was Bishop of East Anglia for 17 years. The first church at Babingley was said to have been built near the beach where he came ashore in the Wash at the beginning of his mission to north-west Norfolk.

The village sign depicts a beaver in a bishop's mitre, grasping a bishop's crook. St Felix sailed up the Babingley river after crossing from Burgundy. His boat got into difficulties and he was saved from drowning, it is said, by a colony of beavers. In gratitude he made the lead beaver a bishop.

I went in search of the 'new' church, built in 1894 as a gift from the Prince of Wales, who became King Edward VII. Made of corrugated iron and pitch pine, and with a thatched roof, it started out as a shining example of benevolent paternalism towards a population of 92 by the new master of Sandringham House. It also served as a parish meeting place.

When I found it, hidden behind trees and rusty railings near the Babingley crossroads, the 'Iron Mission' seemed to be crumbling into history just like its more illustrious predecessor. As traffic thundered past to and from King's Lynn, I pushed through brambles and straggling branches to inspect gravestones erected as recently as the 1970s. I peered through a gap in the church wall where a window used to be and recoiled at the pungent smells of damp and decay. A font, a piano and a chair were discernible through the musty gloom, symbols of a little community's past gratitude for royal patronage and parish celebrations.

Just a few weeks later came news that the Royal Estate was planning to restore the 'Iron Mission' and to find an alternative use for it, possibly as an office or studio.

BACONSTHORPE

—— A downright shifty lawyer who made much of his pile during the Wars of the Roses, Sir John Heydon led the Norfolk field when it came to corruption and arrogance on the grand scale. He even tried to bribe the Speaker of the House of Commons with a £1,000 back-hander.

He put a fair amount of his ill-gotten gains into new property, starting work on a Norfolk manor house in the mid-15th century. Naturally, he didn't apply for the customary licence. The remains of Baconsthorpe Castle, near Holt, still tell fascinating tales of a family's changing fortunes.

There's plenty of fresh air to go with the history after following the English Heritage sign down a long farmyard track north of the village. Two flint-faced gatehouses and parts of the original curtain wall immediately emphasise it was once a handsome building. I returned on a day blessed with clear skies and a sudden rise in temperature. Snowdrops, those brave little harbingers of spring, dotted out a welcome on the banks of the moat. Geese honked their displeasure at human intrusion. Crows shot out of ancient brickwork like erratic smoke, black and twisting, while big molehills forced you to tread carefully across the courtyard.

After a few minutes of imagining what life was like 500 years ago, farm silos, water towers, telegraph poles and planes writing modern names on the sky became the items out of fashion, out of place. Baconsthorpe Castle gives off a grandness, a sense of permanence and pride that lifts it way beyond the 'interesting ruins' department. The period to leave the biggest mark was the 17th century, when it became the centre of a vast sheep run. The place was transformed to house a wool industry.

The outer gatehouse is the most impressive survivor. Built in Elizabethan times for show rather than defiance, it was lived in until 1920 when one of the turrets collapsed. The Heydon family star had waned with the Civil War. Parliament sequestrated what remained of the estates. Soon they were demolishing the Baconsthorpe empire and offering the stone for sale. In 1654, the Heydons put £35 in their dwindling coffers when 18 carts arrived to remove freestone to Felbrigg Hall, near Cromer. Scant consolation in a little bit of Baconsthorpe glory going into the transfer market.

Open all year round with free entrance, this is one of Norfolk's most attractive and underrated sites.

BACTON

────── A gatehouse and a few jagged pieces of masonry do little to convey the wonder and hope which once must have surrounded this corner of Bacton, a coastal settlement better known today for its giant terminal receiving natural gas from the North Sea.

Bromholm Priory was established in 1113 as an offshoot or cell of Castle Acre. In about 1205, its fortunes were transformed when an East Anglian priest who had visited Constantinople gave the Cluniac monks two small pieces of wood which he claimed to be parts of the True Cross. Within a few years miracles were being talked of, and in 1226 Henry III paid the first royal visit to this obscure corner of north-east Norfolk.

The monks began a new series of buildings, parts of which can still be seen. In the 15th century one chronicler wrote that 19 people had their sight restored and no fewer than 39 had been raised from the dead. Sadly the obviously potent relic disappeared in 1537 after it had been sent to Thomas Cromwell in London.

Approached off the B1159 main coast road at Bacton, the ruinous gatehouse bars the way to further remains which rest beside farm buildings. These include sections of the wall of the north and south transepts of the priory and parts of the chapter house, dormitory, refectory and west range.

The Paston family were patrons of Bromholm Priory. In 1466, Sir John Paston died in London as he tried to recover Caister for the Duke of Norfolk. Sir John was brought to the priory to be buried. The funeral was an extravagant affair, and a barber was engaged for five days to smarten up the monks. The priory glazier had to remove two panes of glass to allow the fumes to escape, 'lest the congregation should be suffocated'. Provision was made for 13 barrels of beer, 27 barrels of ale, one barrel of 'great assye' (a very strong drink), a runlet of wine of 15 gallons, plus 15 coombs of malt to be brewed up for the occasion. The country all around was swept for decent chickens. Twenty pounds in gold was changed into small coins 'for showering among the attendant throng'.

BALE

—— Nestling peacefully among trees off the busy Holt-Fakenham road, little Bale is home to one of Norfolk's most colourful legends – and it lives on in a small spinney by the parish church of All Saints.

The Bale Oak was reputed to be over 500 years old when it was cut down and carted off in 1860. At between two and three feet from the base it measured 36 feet in circumference, and one of its branches was 75 feet long. It was possibly the remains of a Celtic or Saxon grove, in which Christians later built their church of All Saints. It stood on the left of the main path outside the church gates.

The oak was showing signs of advanced age by 1632. The churchwardens' accounts of that year state: 'For felling one arme of the oake and carting the same to the cost of the church 5s 0d . . . for the timber carieng & sawing on the pitt.' A record in 1716 says: 'Thomas Bullen sett the two oaks which now stand at the S. west and the N. west corners of the green.' These may have been the evergreen oaks, such a fine feature of Bale today. A note attributed to Norfolk historian Francis Blomefield (1705–1752) reads: 'A Great Oak at Bathele [alias Bale] near the church. Hollow so large that ten or twelve men may stand within it. A cobbler had his shop and lodge there of late and it is or was used for a swinestry.'

In 1795 the Bale Oak was severely pollarded and the Hardys of Letheringsett bought the wood and bark for tanning. It never recovered from this drastic treatment, and a poem was written about the tree in this state. The verse was passed down and there are those who can quote it easily to this day:

Here stand I all in disgrace,
Once the wonder of this place;
My head knocked off, my body dead
And all the virtues of my limbs is fled.
'Tis all my fear that I should fright
The traveller's horse by night.
So cut me down, it's my desire,
Commit me to the blazing fire,
And when you see me burn and smoke
Say 'That's the end of the old Bale Oak'.

The tree had become dangerous by 1860 and as the parish officers would take no responsibility for anyone getting injured, the Lord of the Manor, Sir Willoughby Jones, Bart, had the tree taken down and carted off to Cranmer Hall at Fakenham. The wagons used were decked with flags and the whole town came out to see them pass.

The old pub in Bale was called the Angel and Oak from 1836 to 1845, the Oak Inn during 1879 and the Bale Oak in the 1880s. The fame of the old tree spread, no doubt, when 30 people from Bale left to seek a new life in Canada.

Oaks in the hedgerow of Top Field off Slade Road are said to have been grown from acorns of the Bale Oak. The spinney by the church known as the Bale Oaks, became National Trust property in 1919.

BAWDESWELL

The only church in the region destroyed in a wartime aircraft crash was All Saints at Bawdeswell on 6th November 1944. A Mosquito bomber from No 608 Squadron based at Downham Market was returning from a bombing raid over Germany. It is thought that severe icing trouble caused the pilot, James McLean, to lose control. He and Sergeant Melvyn Tansley were killed as the aircraft crashed on the church, which had been rebuilt in 1845.

A new church was completed ten years later on the site of the old one. It is in classic Colonial style, and one parishioner suggested it would look better in Norfolk, Virginia.

There was a difference of opinion about the spire on the tower. Some parish council members thought it was too much at variance with the Norfolk church tradition and others still feared danger from low-flying aircraft. A special Consistory Court met at Bawdeswell in November 1954, when it was decided to adhere to the architect's original plan. The spire is built of wood with cedar wood tiles surmounted by a copper ball with a weathercock. The church was consecrated by the Bishop of Norwich on 27th September 1955. The fabric cost about £12,000, which came from the War Damage Commission.

Time has silenced the critics and the building now seems at home in its Norfolk setting. On Sunday, 4th November 1990, a special service was held in the church. A plaque made from pieces of the crashed aircraft was dedicated to the two airmen who died in the tragedy. Among those present were Pilot Officer McLean's sister and a Mosquito Squadron Leader who had served at nearby Foulsham. Outside the church is a cross with a small plaque inscribed: 'When the church was destroyed on November 6th, 1944, this cross remained standing on the top of the bell tower. The cross was originally erected in loving memory of John Gurney who died March 29th, 1932.'

BEESTON-NEXT-MILEHAM

There are four Beestons in Norfolk – Beeston St Lawrence, not far from Wroxham; Beeston St Andrew, four miles north-east of Norwich; Beeston Regis, near Sheringham, and Beeston-next-Mileham, in the middle of the county. My preference for the last-named is based on the premise that your heart is where your home is.

I was born and raised there at a time when most families were closely connected with agriculture. Much has changed since I left the village in the early 1960s to pursue a career in journalism, but it still holds a special place in my affections. I return whenever possible, especially to keep in touch with the little primary school where my education began and to pay respects in the churchyard where family and friends are buried.

A white stone memorial in that same churchyard recalls Beeston's most famous son. Jem Mace, the father of modern scientific boxing and one-time world heavyweight champion, was born in the village in 1831, son of the local blacksmith. Apprenticed to a cabinetmaker at Wells on the north Norfolk coast, young Jem boxed at fairs and race meetings before winning national acclaim.

He won the British heavyweight title in 1861 and defended the crown successfully against Tom King after 43 rounds of fierce fighting. King won a return bout and then, after beating American champion John Heenan for the world title, decided to retire. Mace took over and became universally known as world champion after beating Joe Goss. Mace successfully defended his crown twice before retiring. He continued to box in exhibitions.

He died in Liverpool at the age of 79. In later years he was landlord of the Swan public house in Norwich. That white stone memorial was retrieved from a Norwich stonemason's yard and moved to his home village in 1976 by 'A few of his old friends'. Many a smile is raised on noting that across the path is a stone for a Henry Cooper!

If that fails to impress sufficiently, I can always point to the Beeston connection with a world famous man of music.

I was barely six months old when Glenn Miller led his musicians into a giant hangar about a mile from my old homestead. Our local airfield, home to the 392nd Bomb Group, was carved out of farmland between Beeston and Wendling, and so both parishes can claim a slice of aviation and show-biz history. Five B-24s landed on 25th August 1944 and unloaded Glenn Miller's band to entertain US servicemen and their new-found friends. A full house of 300 soon got in the mood. I'm sure I heard music being carried across the meadows as I kicked the blanket off my pram.

BEESTON ST LAWRENCE

—— Souvenirs of dramatic times in a Russia rocked by revolution are included among the treasures of Beeston Hall, built in 1786 in the fashionable Gothic style with a distinctive

Norfolk touch – a facing of knapped flint.

Standing in extensive parkland and overlooking a lake, the hall is open to the public on certain days. The old village not far from Wroxham, self-styled Capital of the Broads, has gone; the population a century ago had dwindled to less than 50. Thomas Preston, who succeeded to the baronetcy late in life on the death of his cousin, brought those souvenirs from Russia back to his family home after a highly eventful career as the British Consul in Ekaterinburg on the eastern slopes of the Ural Mountains. It was there in April 1918 that Czar Nicholas II and his family were brought by revolutionary soldiers to spend the last two months of their lives.

Thomas Preston was implicated in rescue plans and was sentenced to death, but the timely capture of Ekaterinburg by the White Army prevented the sentence from being carried out. The Consul lived to tell the tale to, among others, George V, on his return to England. Among Russian mementos at Beeston Hall are the painting in the Staircase Hall of the Czar's Cossack escort in 1914, and the candelabra, samovar and firescreen in the Dining Room.

Thomas Preston's part in these historic events was in line with a family tradition of service to the country. An earlier Preston was a herald at the court of Charles I, and another an active supporter of William of Orange. It was Jacob Preston, who much preferred his own garden to the wider world of politics, who created Beeston Hall. He acquired his tastes on the Grand Tour and became a Fellow of the Society of Antiquarians. In the 1780s he conceived the idea of demolishing the old hall and rebuilding it in the Gothic style with a local vernacular touch. Sadly, he did not survive to enjoy the results. In November 1787, with work almost done, he was setting out to visit the local house of industry for the poor when he had a heart attack and fell dead from his horse.

BINHAM

Founded in the late 11th century by Pierre de Valoines, nephew of William the Conqueror, Binham Priory had an eventful history under a series of unscrupulous and often scandalous priors. It suffered a siege in 1212 when the poor brethren had to eat bread made from bran and drink water from the rain-pipe. The priory surrendered to Henry VIII's Dissolution of the Monasteries in 1540. The monastic buildings were mostly pulled down, stone being used for other buildings, but the nave of the church continued in use as the parish church.

Today the Priory Church of St Mary and the Holy Cross, to some extent a ruin within a greater ruin, is an inspiring and unique place of worship, especially in the summer months when services are held at the open-air altar. The magnificent west front of the priory church is the first thing to strike visitors, a rich and elaborate example of Early English architecture. The great west window has been bricked up since 1809, but the bas tracery is admirable.

To the south of the church are the remains of the monastic area. Visitors enter through a precinct between the church and the cloister into the monks' outer parlour. Enough remains to give a good impression of the layout of the main buildings. It is possible to identify the chapter house, the warming room with hearth, the refectory, the reredorter or latrines, the cellarer's range and the kitchens.

The shaft of the market cross still stands on the village green in this settlement five miles south-east of Wells. In the reign of Henry I a charter was granted for an annual fair lasting four days and for a weekly market on Wednesdays. Fairs were held until the early 1950s.

 ## BIXLEY

——— Only three miles south-east of Norwich, this parish retains a remarkable air of remoteness as the city's tentacles spread and traffic roars beyond the headlands.

The church is isolated in the fields, but in this case it was a road and not a village that moved away, and you can still trace the line of the old route along the west side of the churchyard. This was, until 1800, the main Norwich to Bungay road. The church is the only one in England dedicated in honour of St

Wandregesilius, Abbot of Fontanelle in Normandy in the 7th century. During the Middle Ages pilgrimages were made to the statue of 'Seynt Wandrede of Biskeley'. This statue was destroyed in 1538, but another was set up in the traditional place to the north of the altar.

There has been a church on this spot since very early times. The building mentioned in the Domesday Book was rebuilt in 1272 by William of Dunwich, a rich man who was Bailiff of Norwich and co-founder with Bishop Suffield of the Great Hospital in the city.

In 1868, Bixley church, with the exception of the embattled western tower, was again rebuilt. A foundation stone used in 1272 was moved inside to a place by the altar. On one face there is a mass dial, showing that it was outside facing south, and on the other a six-line inscription soliciting prayers for the soul of the founder.

Bixley Hall, demolished at the beginning of this century, was a handsome house of three storeys standing in beautiful grounds. In its park, not far from the church, once stood Bixley Oak, an enormous tree for which the sum of £120 was offered during the Napoleonic Wars 'for the use of the navy'.

The list of Bixley rectors goes back to 1294. Longest serving was John of Esterford (1367–1419). He was rector under seven Popes, six Archbishops of Canterbury, five Bishops of Norwich and four Kings of England. Another rector, George Troghleye, died in 1528 owing the Prioress of Carrow three years' rent – three hens!

BLAKENEY

Well-to-do weekenders who enjoy a spot of sailing would appear to dominate the scene at Blakeney, once a port and fishing village beside a tidal creek on the north Norfolk coast. Almost a third of the 600 dwellings are second homes or holiday lets. Most local jobs are casual, seasonal and low paid.

Yet, despite house prices inflated by holiday demand, many local workers still live in the cottages their forefathers built and occupied. These houses have kept their traditional appearance but the interiors have been brought up to modern standards as far as possible.

This decidedly unusual survival of a local community in historic buildings is largely due to the Blakeney Neighbourhood Housing Society, which celebrated its Golden Jubilee in 1996 with 41 cottages under its wing and controlling more than a third of the social housing in Blakeney.

The Society owes its existence to the pioneering efforts of Norah Clogstoun, who settled in the village in 1938 when her husband, a retired Army officer, was offered work at the nearby Weybourne and Stiffkey camps. One of her wartime activities was to carry sandbags to cottages occupied by old folk. The sand was to put out any incendiary bombs that came through the roof. Norah was shocked by the poor condition of many of the houses and the failure of landlords to carry out essential maintenance. Gradually, Norah saw she would have to own the properties if she was going to get results.

When a row of five was put up for auction she bid successfully, and then borrowed the money to pay for them. Then she met a housing manager who outlined the advantages of forming a housing society. In May 1946 she presided at a public meeting when it was decided to form such a society with seven local people elected to a committee of management.

Mrs Clogstoun also foresaw rising demand for holiday homes in the coastal village. Without the Society, Blakeney High Street might have been totally lost to the community. Some villagers found it hard to believe the voluntary committee were not feathering their own nests, but by 1962 feelings of suspicion and hostility had all but disappeared.

Norah Clogstoun died in 1963 knowing the Society had sound finances and a secure future. In recent years Blakeney has benefited from the generosity of those holiday home owners who appreciate the need to help safeguard the local community. Some have bequested cottages to the Society while others have sold to it for a nominal sum.

Blakeney Neighbourhood Housing Society is now widely accepted as a vital element in the community, attracting both local people and incomers as committee members and officers. A rare but valuable example of a new spirit of co-operation in this part of well-heeled Norfolk.

It has been described as 'the finest pyramid in England', and it awaits those who can tear themselves away from the wonders of Blickling Hall for a stroll in the extensive park. A stark, neo-classical pyramid mausoleum in the Great Wood contains the remains of John Hobart, 2nd Earl of Buckinghamshire, and his family.

He became Earl in 1756, ambassador to St Petersburg between 1762 and 1765 and Lord Lieutenant of Ireland for three years from 1777. He died under mysterious circumstances in 1793. The Blickling Hall guide book quotes Horace Walpole as saying that Lord Buckinghamshire 'suffered from gout in his foot, dipped it in cold water and so killed himself.'

During his lifetime he made fashionable alterations to Blickling, employing the skills of the Ivory family (Thomas Ivory built the Assembly Room in Norwich). Modernisations included

Pyramid mausoleum in Blickling Park.

the enchanting Chinese Bedroom with its hand-painted wallpaper and the Peter the Great Room, named after its Russian tapestry of the Czar.

Blickling Hall, built in the 17th century, is now owned by the National Trust. It has extensive gardens and is surrounded by splendid parkland and woodland. Just over a mile west of Aylsham on the B1354, it is signposted off the A140 Cromer road. The pyramid mausoleum is over two miles from the car park – but well worth the walk.

BLO NORTON

Son of the Maharajah Duleep Singh, who bought the Elveden Estate near Thetford in 1863, Prince Frederick Duleep Singh achieved one of his main ambitions by acquiring the beautiful 16th-century moated manor house of Blo Norton Hall.

He moved into his 'dream home' between Thetford and Diss in 1906, and laid out the grounds, including a pillared temple in a wood dedicated to 'The Divine Winds of Heaven'.

Conservative by nature – he refused to have electric light or telephones at Blo Norton – he was a Jacobite by sympathy. His house was hung with portraits of Bonnie Prince Charlie and other Stuarts, while a portrait of Oliver Cromwell was hung head down. His collection of Stuart relics included a pendant containing a piece of the block on which Charles I was executed and a locket with a ringlet of his hair.

It was Prince Frederick who brought his father's body back to his beloved Elveden for burial and the grave of the 'Black Prince' is still a place of pilgrimage for Sikhs. Frederick was educated at Eton and Cambridge and served in both the Suffolk and Norfolk Yeomanry, attaining the rank of major. After gaining his MA in History at Cambridge, he devoted himself to the study of Norfolk's past. A bachelor, he lived at Breckles Hall and Old Buckenham Hall before settling at Blo Norton, where he died in 1926.

Five years earlier he had purchased the Ancient House in Thetford, a 15th-century merchant's house, and gave it to the town for use as a museum. His collection of books can be seen in the local history section of Thetford library.

Blo Norton Hall is privately owned, but the parish church, with a tablet to Prince Frederick, is open.

BODNEY

You might have to work overtime to imagine this tiny settlement of ten cottages and a church, and a population of under 20, caught up in the vast theatre of war. But Bodney's humble grass airfield a few miles from Watton was once a centre of feverish activity.

In the early part of the last war it was a base for the RAF, operating Blenheims. Then in July 1943 it was handed over to the American 8th Air Force and the 352nd Fighter Group moved in. By April 1944, the Group had made the switch to the Mustang, and it was one of these aircraft that crashed into the control tower at Bodney in the early hours of D-Day, killing the pilot. In a combat career lasting until May 1945, the 352nd Group flew 420 operational missions and were responsible for the destruction of over 800 enemy aircraft.

Other notable deeds carried out from this Norfolk outpost included taking part in the first bombing missions to land in what was the Soviet Union and being sent to Belgium to help counter the German offensive in the Ardennes, known as the Battle of the Bulge.

In 1980 the 352nd Fighter Group Association was formed in the USA and reunions have been held both there and at Bodney. Some of the original accommodation units are still occupied by Army personnel using the adjoining Stanford Battle Area.

During the French Revolution Bodney Hall, then owned by the Tasburgh family, was host to a community of French nuns. Several of them are buried in the churchyard.

BOOTON

It still comes as a surprise, no matter how many times you set eyes on the Cathedral of the Fields at Booton on the outskirts of

Cathedral of the Fields at Booton, a stirring monument to Victorian enthusiasm.

Reepham. 'A bit like finding a symphony orchestra in a tumbledown barn' is typical of reaction to this many-pinnacled parish church of St Michael, startling and unorthodox, with twin towers set cornerwise. A magnificent monument to Victorian enthusiasm.

It was created by Whitwell Elwin, Booton's rector for 50 years. He began rebuilding the village church in the 1870s, his design including details from as far afield as Venice and the early Coptic churches in Egypt.

With no architectural training and no ability as a draughtsman, Elwin was still confident he was building for eternity. The mason carrying out repairs a century later was eloquent in his praise for the work. Materials used were limestone from Bath and black knapped flints from the beach at Mundesley on the Norfolk coast. Leading architect Edwin Lutyens found the use of materials unsympathetic and wrong, but remarked in public that Booton's church was 'very naughty, but built in the right spirit'.

Booton was never a big parish. Maintaining so large a building became increasingly difficult, especially when falls of laminating stone put at risk visitors attracted by the towers and minarets. St Michael's was deemed to be pastorally redundant and in 1987 it was vested in the Redundant Churches Fund. Occasional services are held, and our family has enjoyed a Nativity play among the pews.

Elwin, who died on 1st January 1900, also edited the *Quarterly Review*, the influential High Tory journal, and was a friend to many contemporary writers including Scott and Thackeray. Elwin is credited with bringing the *Review*'s attitude up to date, improving the quality of its writing and extending the range of its contributors. It was the volume of editorial correspondence that forced the Post Office to install the letter box at Booton.

BRANCASTER STAITHE

A fishing village since Roman times, Brancaster Staithe still harbours a few men earning a precarious living from the North Sea. A straggling one-street community along the edge of the salt marshes, it is a popular spot between Wells and Hunstanton, so much so that about half its dwellings are holiday homes. Even so, some families who made their living here when it was a small port and fishing village are still in evidence. When newcomers and holidaymakers request a good smuggling yarn or two, they are introduced to William Hotching . . .

A smuggler who ended his days as an honest man selling fish in surrounding villages, Hotching kept a beer house named the Hat and Feathers in the 1860s in the easterly portion of what is now The Hoe, backing onto the marshes. He owned a lugger and had a share in a 50 ft cutter, and these would meet Dutch boats out at sea and bring in cargoes of tobacco strip. Hotching built a cellar behind the beer house and also had a big hiding place behind a chimney. At other times he hid his tobacco in either marl or chalk pits in a dip off the road to Burnham Market. This later became known as Thieves' Hole. If tides dictated a daylight operation he would organise events like a bowling competition at the White Horse pub so all the fishermen and their families would be occupied.

Hotching and his partners were caught in a trap at King's Lynn. As he was delivering a load of tobacco to a new client, the excise men pounced under the South Gate arch of the town. He and his fellow smugglers were convicted and fined £840 each or six months in prison. They chose prison. When he came out, Hotching decided to go straight despite overtures to return to bad old habits. He was a successful shellfish merchant for the rest of his life. His son Sheldrake, known as Shelley, often regaled his fellow villagers at Brancaster Staithe with tales of his father's smuggling adventures. Shelley spent his working days as a policeman.

A building with standing room for just two people has been officially listed to be preserved at Brancaster Staithe. The oldest Automobile Association telephone box in East Anglia is a Grade II listed building in a lay-by off the busy A149. The sentry-style black box is over 40 years old and one of just a few originals kept in working order in the country. Locals deny that it is used to contact the excise men in the event of any smuggling!

BRESSINGHAM

——— Many Norfolk parishes parade new village halls, community centres and sports facilities, reflecting big changes in what country life can offer these days. But some places still lean heavily on history to meet their recreational needs. Bressingham, near Diss, provides a colourful example with a village hall that is also a Grade II listed building steeped in the past.

A converted threshing barn, it was once part of the moated

Priory Manor of Bressingham, a sub-priory of that at Old Buckenham. Main clues to the past are several old priory buildings, remains of the moat and other places in the locality thought to have been part of the outbuildings or farms belonging to the priory. Within the moated area stand Thatchers, believed to be the old Prior's House, The Highlands and The Elms. Occupied until the 1970s as two cottages, The Elms was probably built as a new home for the prior, but the Dissolution came before it could be used as such.

The village hall lies within the moated area of the priory boundary. It dates from well before the reign of Henry VIII. In the 1950s local farmer George Adam Aves gave the building and the land it stands on as gifts to the village. Funds were raised initially to convert the old barn into a meeting place for Bressingham.

Demands have grown along with the village population, but needs to modernise have had to be placed alongside the importance of preserving precious heritage. A rare but exciting challenge for this south Norfolk community.

BROOKE

——— Special celebrations were held here in 1968 to mark the 200th anniversary of the birth in the village of one of the country's outstanding surgeons. A street in Brooke, seven miles south of Norwich, now bears his name – Astley Cooper Place – to go with the statue erected to him in St Paul's Cathedral.

Surgery was in his blood, for his grandfather and uncle were surgeons of note. When he was only 21, Astley Paston Cooper was appointed demonstrator at St Thomas' Hospital, a post he filled brilliantly. As his fame as a lecturer grew his private practice flourished until it became the largest any surgeon has ever had. In 1802 this son of the Rector of Brooke was elected Fellow of the Royal Society and his income in one year reached a staggering £21,000. For one operation carried out at the peak of his fame, a rich West Indian planter tossed him a thousand guineas in his nightcap!

He became Professor of Comparative Anatomy to the Royal

College of Surgeons, and in 1817 performed his historic operation of tying the abdominal aorta for aneurysm. He received a baronetcy for operating on George IV who had a small tumour in the scalp, and many other honours and successes followed. When he died at 73, Sir Astley was buried in the chapel at Guy's Hospital.

BURGH CASTLE

──── The best preserved Roman monument in Norfolk used to be over the border! Until local government reorganisation in 1974, this fascinating site was part of Suffolk. Burgh Castle was one of ten defensive fortresses built mostly in the 3rd century to defend Britain against increasingly frequent attacks from Anglo-Saxon pirates.

The fort, known then as Gariannonum, was well situated to provide a base for a part of the Roman fleet to patrol the estuary and the surrounding seas. It overlooks the marshland stretching from Yarmouth to Acle, where a salt-water estuary was open to the sea until it was blocked in the Saxon period by the sand spit on which Yarmouth now stands. There are three surviving walls about 15 feet high. Large bastions have been added to each corner. In the 7th century, King Sigebert of the East Angles gave Burgh Castle to St Fursey, who came as a missionary from Ireland in AD 633. He set up a monastery here as part of the process of converting the Saxons to Christianity.

The site is open to the public. Turn off the A143 Bungay-Yarmouth road near Belton. Park at the church and follow signs to the fort.

BURGH ST PETER

──── It looks as if a child has been busy with a box of bricks. A series of cubes piled one on top of the other in diminishing size makes up one of the most remarkable church towers in the country. Soaring above the desolate marshes at the end of a long track from Haddiscoe, it has been described variously as a folly, a

'Tower of Cubes' at Burgh St Peter.

monstrosity and a pyramid. One thing is certain – you can't ignore it! One explanation for the unusual shape could be that the surrounding land being marshy would not hold a conventional tower. Its base, however, is part of the original 16th-century tower which did fall down.

St Mary's tower serves as a memorial or mausoleum to Samuel Boycott who built it in 1793 as a replacement for the earlier tower destroyed in a storm. He lies buried beneath it. The Boycotts were rectors at St Mary's from 1764 until 1899, and there are brass memorials to the family in this church on the river Waveney, with Suffolk on the opposite bank.

BURSTON

The longest strike in English history, lasting from 1914 until just before the Second World War, was sparked by affection and respect for two schoolteachers in a small south Norfolk village. It was a genuine expression of grass-roots democracy.

In 1911 Tom and Kitty Higdon took up teaching posts in Burston. They were soon accepted into the community, where they were working in a desperately poor environment with low wages and cramped housing, while the school premises were in an appalling condition. When Tom Higdon became involved in trade union activities and the couple tried to improve conditions in the school, they met fierce opposition from the Rev. Charles Tucker-Eland, rector and chairman of the school governors and self-appointed upholder of the social and economic status quo. The events that followed, bizarre and ultimately violent, have become known as the Burston School Strike, a strike started by children when their teachers were dismissed. It involved socialist leaders and trade unionists across the country and captured the support of the radical press.

The Higdons were evicted from the school house. Their cottage was attached to the school building and occupancy went with the job. A Strike School Fund was set up and over £1,000 was collected which enabled the Higdons to buy a piece of land and build a school of their own on the village green. The foundation stone was laid in May 1917, and a large contingent of supporters from London

Burston Strike School, now a museum.

included Sylvia Pankhurst, the famous suffragette. The Strike School continued until 1939, the year of Tom Higdon's death. Kitty, five years older than her husband, was in sad decline when Tom died. Several times she was found wandering the lanes at night, saying she was waiting for him to return home from a union meeting. She died in 1946, and both are buried in Burston churchyard.

Before moving to Burston, the Higdons had been teaching for eight years at another Norfolk school in the village of Wood Dalling about 40 miles away. Despite good reports from school inspectors, they were dismissed because of 'friction' between them and the school managers.

The Burston Strike School is now a museum. In recent years there has been a revival of the rallies and marches first held on Burston Green in the 1920s and 30s. For many, the Burston

School Strike ranks alongside the exploits of the Tolpuddle Martyrs as one of the key developments in the fight for independence by the rural working class.

BYLAUGH

—— A Grade I listed ruin on the hill above the village wears a sinister look as darkness falls. In daylight you can spot the Nissen huts and workyards, remnants of the last war when the house was used for military purposes. Most of the original parkland has been ploughed up. Bylaugh Hall has been a ruin since the early 1950s. There have been several plans to restore it and to build holiday hideaways or retirement homes around it. But there it stands, stark and apparently forgotten behind the boundary wall. Bylaugh is five miles north-east of Dereham, and just like Belaugh near Wroxham is pronounced Beloe or Beelar.

Sir John Lombe is reputed to have won the Bylaugh estate from Richard Lloyd by gambling, and the Lloyd family nurse promptly put a curse on Lombe and the house he intended to build, saying that it would last a mere century. The house was completed in 1852. It was in the Tudor style of brick faced with limestone and enriched by carefully carved detail. The house was partially demolished in 1952 owing to delays in the awarding of a preservation order. Perhaps the Lloyd family nurse was watching from a distance . . .

Some see it now as a magnificent ruin, perhaps more beautiful in desolation than ever it was as an inhabited home. The walls still stand, but the roof and most of the woodwork have gone. The stone frames for the former windows are erect on their parapets, but inside the jungle is taking over as ivy wreathes the classical reliefs and medallions.

CAISTER-ON-SEA

—— One of the most telling lines in lifeboat history came at the opening of an inquest at Caister, next door to Yarmouth, in the dark days of 1901. It followed the tragedy of the lifeboat

Caister's marble memorial to the lifeboat victims of the 1901 disaster.

Beauchamp, with the loss of nine of the crew. The lifeboat had been launched to go to the aid of a stranded vessel in heavy seas. After repeatedly being washed back onto the beach the boat capsized.

It was suggested to one of the survivors, James Haylett, that the lifeboatmen could have given up their mission and have been returning to the beach. Haylett replied in defiant tones: 'Caister men never turn back!', sentiments synonymous with the spirit of all village crews ever since.

For his part in the rescue of the three survivors, James Haylett was awarded the RNLI Gold Medal which he received from King Edward VII at Sandringham House in 1902. The vessel the lifeboat had been launched to assist on that wild November night is thought to have been a Lowestoft smack, which managed to lay an anchor in deep water where she remained until daylight and was then seen to sail away, apparently unaware of the drama that had unfolded on the beach only a few hours before.

It was estimated that up to 20,000 people attended the funeral of the nine beachmen and a public appeal raised almost £12,000 for the widows and 44 fatherless children. A large memorial, carved in Italian marble, was erected in a corner of the village cemetery. The east window of the parish church was renewed in 1903 and dedicated to the disaster.

The *Beauchamp* had been to the aid of 81 vessels and saved 146 lives during the nine years it was stationed at Caister. Following the accident it was withdrawn from lifeboat service, and was used for many years as a pleasure craft on the Norfolk Broads. In 1961 the owner offered the boat to the proposed maritime museum for East Anglia and it was stored for several years at the rear of Gorleston library, awaiting restoration. But eventually deterioration of the hull and strong views held about preservation by the Caister beachmen led to the remains being broken up. Caister's RNLI station closed in 1969, but the tradition continued with the launching of a volunteer rescue service, unique in the country.

CALIFORNIA

A 'gold-rush' in the latter part of the 19th century brought a familiar name to the Norfolk coastline. California is the name of what is now a bungalow settlement and holiday haunt just north of Caister-on-Sea. It is so called because of a find by 'pawkers' – Norfolk for beachcombers – of a hoard of gold coins. They were of various reigns from Henry VIII to Charles I. Archaeologist Charles Green thought they must have been buried during the Civil War in a now-forgotten hamlet destroyed by coastal erosion, the hoard being exposed again and scattered in the sand by another scour of tides 200 years later.

In any event, one of these 'pawkers', a fisherman from nearby Scratby, found as many as 90 coins – and bought himself a new boat with the proceeds.

CARBROOKE

A house for the Knights Templars was founded here by Maud, Countess of Clare, in the 12th century, the only one of its kind in Norfolk. Standing near the south porch of the parish church of St Peter and St Paul and looking south-east you can spot grass-covered lumps and bumps, all that is left of the 'commandery of Kerbrook'. During periods of extreme dryness outlines of buildings can be seen as bleached areas on the grass. What used to be fish ponds, providing food for the monks, have had water in them at times during the past few years.

Ordinary monks lived in monasteries, but the fighting monks were in preceptories or commanderies. These flourished until Henry VIII ordered their dissolution. Under Edward II, the Templars' order had been suppressed and their lands given to the Knights of St John of Jerusalem. An important part of the work of the English commanderies was to collect alms and gifts. After keeping what was necessary to support the local community, the commander sent the balance to the Priory of Clerkenwell in London. From here the net total was forwarded to the Convent in Jerusalem.

In the church of this parish near Watton are two grave slabs in front of the high altar carrying the 'cross patee' of the Knights Templars, the cross in which the four limbs expand outwards from a narrow centre. These are likely to be the graves of the foundress and one of the younger sons, and so could be the earliest burial slabs in Norfolk, dating from the early 13th century.

Norfolk's oldest primary school at Carleton Rode, five miles from Attleborough, received its first pupils in 1822. There were fees to be paid for those who could afford it, about one old penny a week. It was not until 1891 that parents were given the right to demand free education.

Discipline was strict and conditions basic, but for children in this village it was a chance few in rural East Anglia shared at the time. Thanks to the church authorities, an education was to be provided for local youngsters. The rector had come up with the land just across the road from All Saints' parish church and Carleton Rode Church School was built. Today that single-storey flint building with a slate roof remains at the heart of the extended and modernised school building.

From 1863 it became obligatory for the headteacher to record day-to-day events and the rituals of school life in the school log. Now those three volumes provide a fascinating insight over several generations of youngsters in a constantly-changing rural society. These records are kept at the village school and can be viewed by appointment. A history of the school turned into a village best-seller.

Limited accommodation prompted the Rev. John Cholmeley MA to have the school enlarged in 1872 for 150 children, average attendance being about 60. The log tells how illness was rife, resulting in many days away from school. In October 1866 children were off with 'hooping cough', and on another occasion the mistress was unwell and 'children left to their own responsibility'. In February 1878 fees were doubled to 2d a week, and the following month the rector told the children of farmers and tradesmen his new rate would be 3d. On the following Monday he recorded: 'Sent 49 children home as they only brought the usual 1d'.

The school history notes that in January 1878 an invention called the telephone was demonstrated to Queen Victoria. It was to be 1975 before Carleton Rode Primary School had its own. A £92,000 extension opened in November 1997 pointed to a confident future, giving the school a third classroom as well as enabling the provision of a library in a former teaching area for the 61 youngsters on the register. Four years earlier the school got a new gymnasium.

CASTLE RISING

Strange to think this used to be a rotten borough! One of Norfolk's most attractive villages, Castle Rising lives in a world of its own off the King's Lynn to Sandringham road, steeped in history and compliments for the way it is looked after.

A splendid mediaeval cross on a flight of steps stands on the small green which was once a market place. The Norman church peers down on Jacobean almshouses. Charm at every turn, and to crown it all the ruined castle with the row of Scotch firs providing a romantic aspect. Queen Isabella, Edward III's mother, was locked up here in 1330 following her banishment for aiding her lover Roger Mortimer in the murder of Edward II.

Glorious ruins at Castle Rising.

Even so, her time in Castle Rising seems to have been spent in relative comfort, as she received visits from Edward III and his son, the Black Prince.

Across the road from the church the Hospital of the Holy and Undivided Trinity is almost exactly as it was when Henry Howard, Earl of Northampton, ancestor of the present squire, built it in 1614 as an almshouse for 20 spinsters. It is a low brick building with little towers round a quadrangle with mowed lawns and flowers round each old lady's door. The chapel has the old pews and altar table, and there is more Jacobean furniture in the dining hall. The residents go to church in long red cloaks bearing the Howard badge and pointed black hats as they have done since the foundation.

Only women of good character have been eligible for entry over the centuries: 'No common beggar, harlot, scold, drunkard, haunter of taverns, inns and alehouses.' Recent improvements in facilities led to the number being reduced to nine. A narrow staircase beside the gateway leads up to the treasury, with its original panelling, where stands the iron-bound chest which once held the hospital funds. The Trinity Hospital is occasionally open to the public.

CASTON

An attractive and well-kept green is at the heart of this village about four miles from Watton – and it is at the north-east corner of the green that you will find what remains of the village cross. It was built in the late 15th century. Only the base survives, but it is a base of some substance. Unlike any other in Norfolk, it stands about six feet in height and consists of three steps. The top step, which formed the socket, is square and has blank arcading on each side made up of two cinquefoils in the centre and two small trefoils each side. The middle step is octagonal and the lower one circular.

The purpose of the cross is unclear. It may have been a market cross, although traditionally it has been linked with the hospitality and spiritual care received by pilgrims as they made their way to the shrine of Our Lady at Walsingham. Caston, apparently, was on one of the ancient routes to Walsingham and the pilgrims are thought to have had their refectory at Church Farm House, whose north wall bears similar blank arcading to that of the base of the cross and is of the same date. They may also have formed a chapel here.

In the 1950s, when a trench was being dug close to the base of the cross on the northern side, parts of two skeletons were discovered.

CAWSTON

A couple of well-known local politicians allowed a spot of name-calling to fester and then spill over into a deadly feud. The Duel Stone, a short pillar surmounted by an urn, stands on the outskirts of the village of Cawston, north-west of Norwich, to mark the fatal encounter of 1698. Sir Henry Hobart of Blickling Hall represented King's Lynn in the last parliament of Charles II and supported the revolution against James II. Hobart's opponent, Oliver Le Neve of nearby Great Witchingham Hall, was a Tory who had inherited his wealth from a rich uncle. The Whigs were returned to power in 1695 with Hobart in full support. Electioneering had proved financially draining for him and he was forced to sell off some of the family estates to pay his backers.

Another election in 1698 brought Hobart's downfall. He failed to get re-elected and returned crestfallen to Blickling to lick his wounds. Then came reports that Oliver Le Neve was spreading rumours to discredit him, one of them suggesting Hobart had been a coward in Ireland during the crusade with William III, and that this was the real reason he had lost his Norfolk seat. Hobart challenged Le Neve to a duel. A letter came back denying the accusation, but then Hobart insulted Le Neve in public. This time the response was fighting talk.

They met at Cawston Heath on 20th August 1698. Hobart, the better swordsman, wounded his opponent in the arm. However, the left-handed Le Neve thrust his sword deep into his rival's stomach, and Hobart died the next day.

Lady Hobart and friends called for revenge. Le Neve fled to Holland, a price on his head, but eventually returned to stand trial. He was acquitted of any blame, but life after the trial was packed with misfortune. Le Neve's wife died in 1704. He married Elizabeth Sheffield in 1707, but she died three months later. In 1711 a tragic Le Neve died, just a few months after the death of his only son.

The Duel Stone is on the road to Norwich, just before the junction with the B1145.

CLAXTON

Anne of Cleves, one of Henry VIII's more fortunate wives, is the biggest name linked with Claxton Castle, seven miles south-east of Norwich. Tradition asserts that she not only owned the castle built in the 14th century, but also lived there for some time. Now all that remains of the brick and flint building put up by William de Kerdiston is a length of the south wall about 130 feet long with six round bastions, and an isolated pier about 20 yards to the north-west, probably part of the eastern entrance gateway, as what look like portcullis grooves can be discerned in the brickwork. There are traces of a deep moat around the whole site and a four-acre paddock with surrounding wall foundations was evidently a bailey.

The castle had several illustrious owners, earls and dukes of Suffolk including the de la Poles, Thomas Howard and Charles Brandon. Even so, none were likely to have lived there, having bigger properties elsewhere in the region.

William de Kerdiston, builder of the castle, was a wealthy man and a valiant soldier. In 1340 he took part in an expedition into Flanders with ten men at arms and ten archers. Probably as a reward for his services he obtained a grant of a market and fair at Claxton, a valuable and coveted privilege in those days. William must have known Geoffrey Chaucer for their families would seem to have been connected; William's granddaughter married Thomas, the son of the poet. Claxton Castle is referred to several times in the *Paston Letters*, that great Norfolk collection of family correspondence (see the Fersfield and Mautby entries).

The owners of the manor house nearby are usually happy to

welcome those with a particular interest in the castle for a closer inspection. The manor itself probably dates from the early 1700s.

CLEY-NEXT-THE-SEA

——— At the heart of an impressive linked chain of nature reserves on the north Norfolk coast, Cley was once a small town and busy port. Natural silting and deliberate land reclamation have left this picturesque village accessible only to small craft – but it is often awash with birdwatchers gathering to observe rare migrant species.

Visitors in search of the highly unusual would also do well to take a close look at some Cley buildings. The old Custom House, now a private home, was built in 1680, had a new front added in 1729 and was in use until 1853. The property on the corner of Town Yard and Holt Road is known as 'The Barn'. It was built in the early 1700s and was originally known as 'The Town House', providing accommodation for eight male and eight female vagabonds. It became a cattle shed and was bought and converted into a pleasant home in 1970. Whalebone House, formerly a shop, has outer walls decorated with sheep vertebrae. Dominating the centre of the village is Cley Windmill, a Grade II listed building built as a cornmill at the beginning of the 19th century and in operation until 1920.

The splendid parish church of St Margaret looks over the green and the Glaven valley. Many visitors might wonder why such a dominant building is on the edge of the community. Well, on 1st September 1612 a fire destroyed 117 houses in the area of Newgate Green below the church. Happily, there were no human casualties. There were also the effects of the harbour silting up due to natural growth of the shingle bank. Landowners embanked the marshes to provide more grazing land, and the centre of the village moved away from the church to be nearer deep water where new quays could be built.

Over 400 acres of marshland on the eastern side of the village were bought by the Norfolk Naturalists' Trust in 1926, and the area has become a bird centre of international importance. Even so, perhaps the rarest 'species' spotted in Cley this century carried the names Umtata, Umgeni, Umvolosi and Umona. These names of Zulu origin were given to homes in the village, travelling all the way from territories, townships and rivers in South Africa from Zimbabwe down to Cape Province. They were also names of ships and originated with the Rennie Line which operated a joint service to Natal with ships belonging to Bullard King and Company. The fleet was acquired in 1919 by the Union Castle Line, and the names found their way to Cley when a Captain Lewis, who had sailed in the fleet, bought and built properties in the village. At the last count, two of these Zulu names had survived on the main coast road.

The bulk of the early trade from the port of Cley was with the Low Countries, but as the harbour continued to silt up this international business declined and coastal trade increased. Cley was a major outlet for the farm produce of north Norfolk with cargoes of barley, malt, fish, wheat, beer, peas and beeswax going to London and the north-east ports. Another interesting export was oysters. The *Norfolk Chronicle* reported in July 1836: 'Many hundred tons of oysters have been caught off Cley, where there are very extensive beds, during the last season and sold to Kent dealers at less than sixpence a bushel.' Cley's decline as a port was sealed by the coming of the railway to nearby Holt in 1884. Merchants realised they could transport their goods faster and cheaper, and trading ships all but vanished from the local scene. It was time for the tourist trade to take over.

COCKTHORPE

While Burnham Thorpe and Lord Nelson usually take the glory when it comes to Norfolk and seafaring exploits, the little village of Cockthorpe has plenty of scope to demand top honours.

No less than three distinguished admirals of the 17th century have connections with Cockthorpe, just off the coast road at Stiffkey. Sir Cloudesley Shovell and Sir John Narborough were christened at All Saints' church, while Sir Christopher Myngs, baptised at Salthouse, is thought to have spent the early part of his life at Cockthorpe.

Often described as Norfolk's other Nelson, Cloudesley Shovell took the legendary ladder from cabin boy to admiral, his early rise in the Navy coinciding with William of Orange's ascent to the English throne. He went on to distinguish himself above all in the War of the Spanish Succession, which established Britain as a great power. He died in 1707 and is buried in Westminster Abbey.

John Narborough (1640–1688) was involved in the Battle of Sole Bay off Southwold in Suffolk in 1672, and promoted to rear-admiral and knighted the following year. After distinguished Mediterranean service he was posted to the West Indies where he caught a fever and died.

Christopher Myngs (1625–1666) took part in the Battle of Lowestoft, opening battle of the second Dutch War. He was knighted after a decisive victory for the English. In April 1666, he hoisted the flag on the *Victory*, and so became the first Norfolk admiral to be connected with a ship of that name. (Not, of course, the same ship: Nelson's *Victory* was launched in 1765.) During the first days of June, the Dutch and English fleets fought one of the toughest and longest battles in history. The English suffered a heavy defeat which was to be reversed only a few weeks later at the Battle of Orford Ness. Myngs did not live to see it.

The *Victory* did not take part in the first three days of fighting of what is now called the Four Days' Battle. When Myngs did get involved he was shot through the throat. Another bullet passed through his neck and so he became the first of two British admirals of Norfolk stock to be shot and mortally wounded aboard a ship called the *Victory*.

The three admirals with Cockthorpe connections underline Norfolk's claim to have been home to more remarkable seamen than any other county in Britain.

COLTISHALL

—— Commuters and summer visitors have transformed this large Broadland village into a dormitory for Norwich since the last war. Relatively cheap housing and the development of the nearby RAF station brought a steady flow of changes following the break-up of Coltishall's traditional rural economy of farming, malting and boatbuilding.

Victorian Coltishall was built on malt, employing more than 100 men in 18 malthouses along the banks of the Bure with thousands of tons sold to breweries at home and abroad each year. Some was even made into Guinness. The industry had modest beginnings with the earliest malthouses, believed to have been built in the 17th century, supplying small parish breweries. The 19th century saw an unprecedented growth in demand for malt for newly-developed urban breweries all over Britain and this, coupled with the development of efficient river transport, created the conditions in which Coltishall's role could flourish.

Maltsters formed a large working-class community at the heart of village life. They were rough and tough men expected to carry 16 stone sacks of barley as a matter of course. Toiling for long periods close to kilns kept at a constant 220 degrees Fahrenheit, they drank large quantities of beer before going to work to prevent dehydration. Eight or nine pints before breakfast was quite normal when malting started at dawn.

Malting at Coltishall reached its peak before the turn of this century. Production was concentrated at the larger complexes in Anchor Street, White Lion Road and near the Rising Sun and London Tavern. But local malthouses were exposed as uneconomic after the First World War, and they fell victim to the larger plants built beside main line railways in other parts of the county. The last Coltishall malthouses were closed in the winter of 1926–27. They were demolished, converted to residential use or made into greenhouses and garden stores. One was used as a swimming pool, another as a granary. The former maltings next to the bridge leading into the village were turned into an abattoir.

Maltsters were among the first converts of the Salvation Army, which sought to stamp out drunkenness and rowdy behaviour by holding open-air meetings beside the Rising Sun and King's Head. Sixteen wayward souls were 'saved' at the first service in 1885, conducted by three Salvationists who had marched all the way from Norwich.

COSTESSEY

Hailed as Norfolk's own Windsor Castle, Costessey Hall was a palatial dream destined to face an ignoble end on the outskirts of Norwich. Bushes and brambles now invade the ruined domain of the Stafford Jerninghams by the 18th fairway at Costessey Park Golf Club. The graffiti-scarred walls of the former kitchen block rise towards the sky and an empty belfry now plays host to a gaggle of pigeons. Ivy-smothered remains of a grand illusion born of grand ambition.

Of the many grand Norfolk houses which have disappeared down the years, some without trace, none combine to such monumental effect the epic vision and tragic fate of this extraordinary creation.

The history of Costessey Hall is inextricably tied to the rise and fall of the Jerningham dynasty. It is a story of status, social snobbery and extravagant ambitions which has its roots in Tudor England and the decision by Queen Mary to grant Sir Henry Jernegan the Manor of Costessey with its 22 sub-manors for services rendered. Within nine years, Sir Henry, having changed his surname to Jerningham, was established in a new hall built south of the river Tud. For the next 260 years, the splendid hall, built in the shape of an E, remained the family seat, but by the mid-18th century the descendants of Sir Henry were casting envious eyes towards grander titles.

As a result of the marriage of Sir George Jerningham and Mary Plowden, niece and heiress of the last Earl of Stafford, the family laid claim to the Baronry of Stafford. A number of petitions were made in vain until in 1824 Sir George Jerningham, the 7th Baronet, found a willing ally in King George IV. The following year saw his elevation to the Stafford title – and the beginning of one of the greatest ego-trips in Norfolk history. The new Lady Stafford decided the old hall was not grand enough for a Baron, and it was at her insistence that her husband set about building a more palatial place. It was simply far larger than they could ever hope to afford. When the hall was put up for sale in 1913, the kitchen, banqueting hall and conservatory had not been completed. Many bedrooms were never fitted out as large sections of hand-carved oak wall panels were never put up.

None of this prevented the incomplete mansion hosting a succession of lavish parties, the most glittering of which was staged in 1866 in honour of the Prince and Princess of Wales.

By early 1914 the dream palace was no more than an empty shell. The war brought a brief but calamitous stay of execution as the hall and park became an infantry training ground. When renewed efforts to sell were made at the end of the war there was no interest, and it was bought by a demolition contractor for between £4,000 and £5,000. Over the course of the next 30 years the great hall was gradually reduced to rubble, until only remnants of the Thornbury Tower and the belfry block remained. In time, the tower collapsed leaving only a single ragged reminder of the hall's former grandeur.

A final irony – where the hall could be lawfully destroyed in what now seems like little more than an officially sanctioned act of vandalism, the ruin is protected after being classified by the Department of the Environment.

COUNTY SCHOOL

A bold Victorian adventure in the heart of the Norfolk countryside is recalled by the name County School. It was the brainchild of Joseph Lloyd Brereton, whose father was Rector of Little Massingham for 47 years. Joseph succeeded him in 1867, and that led to the birth of the Norfolk County School on the outskirts of North Elmham.

His project interested many leading figures of the time and the Prince of Wales, later King Edward VII, became the school's patron. Despite its name, boys came from all parts of the country and abroad. By 1881 there were over one hundred of them with fees of 40 guineas a time. The school was on the map and Brereton aimed to get it on the railway line. The branch from Wroxham was joined to the Dereham-Fakenham section of the Great Eastern Railway at Broome Green, and in 1884 County School station was opened.

But the school did not flourish and it closed in 1895. At the end of the century the place caught the attention of E. H. Watts, a rich London shipowner and a keen admirer of Dr Barnardo. Through

Trains run again at County School.

his generosity and that of his son the old school was reopened as Watts Naval Training School. That's how it stayed until 1953. Years of uncertainty followed before the school buildings were demolished.

County School has been restored as a tourist attraction with tracks relaid and trains running. Enthusiasts hope to open the line again to North Elmham and then on to Dereham and Wymondham. In fact, County School is in the parish of Bintree, but is well signposted on the road from Guist into North Elmham.

There are a few pointers to the past. The former school chapel has been converted into a private home and one or two other houses also remain. Hidden about halfway up the drive ascending towards the site of the school after leaving the level crossing and station is a tiny cemetery. It contains headstones of about 16 boys who died within the vicinity of the school between 1904 and 1909. Aged from 11 to 14, it appears some had been recaptured after attempting to run away.

———— A drinking trough would appear to be a rather lacklustre memorial to the man who thought up the name 'Poppyland' and made the district around Cromer so fashionable for holidays. But perhaps Clement Scott would have been embarrassed by anything too extravagant, especially as he had deep regrets about the marvellous advertising job he had done!

Scott's articles in the *Daily Telegraph*, coupled with the opening of the railway, helped make Cromer a popular resort. He arrived in town in August 1883, but discovered a place more to his liking during a ramble along the clifftop. Sidestrand, with its crumbling cliffs and fields dotted with poppies, became the haven of peace he had been yearning for.

His articles from 'Poppyland' caught the imagination of the public and also lured literary personalities to the area. The eminent Victorian poet Algernon Charles Swinburne and his friend Theodore Watts-Dunton led the way. Scott continued to make the journey for 15 years, not only in summer. He wrote his famous poem 'The Garden of Sleep' while standing in the old churchyard by the church tower at Sidestrand at Christmas in 1885. It became a ritual to see in the New Year from the same spot, reading the poem as a reminder of the first flush of discovery and, in some ways, as a lament for what his publicity had done.

He wrote in 1890: 'The Cromer that we visit now is not the Cromer I wrote about a few years ago as my beloved Poppyland.' It seemed he felt the area to be doomed, often wishing he had kept it to himself to prevent it from turning into 'Bungalow Land'. Clearly those sentiments had reached Cromer Council by 1909 when they were far from unanimous in supporting the idea of a memorial.

The secretary to the Metropolitan Drinking Fountain and Cattle Trough Association, one Captain Smith, had again written to the council. One member doubted it should be referred to as a fountain when in fact it was a cattle drinking trough. 'Unfortunately', said Captain Smith in his letter, 'the fountain and trough has already been dispatched with the inscription placed on it.' It can be seen today at what many regard as the entrance to Poppyland at the junction of the Overstrand and Northrepps road: 'To Clement Scott, who by his pen immortalised "Poppyland", erected by many friends, November 1909.'

DENVER

—— The Great Denver Sluice complex, three miles from Downham Market, stands as a triumphant example of modern engineering and the application of millions of pounds of capital. But many forget how a Dutchman built the first sluice here around 350 years ago as part of a scheme to drain the fenlands owned by the Earl of Bedford.

Cornelius Vermuyden was the man behind probably the boldest land reclamation programme in England. He may have picked up early experience in Zeeland before he came to this country from Holland in 1621. He was knighted by Charles I in 1629. Then came his major work on the drainage of the Fens, a vast marshy area covering parts of Cambridgeshire, Lincolnshire and Norfolk. He was appointed chief engineer for this project by the Earl of Bedford and 13 'other adventurers' financing the scheme. Between 1634 and 1655, despite strong opposition from many inhabitants, he reclaimed thousands of acres of fenland by cutting the Bedford and Hundred Foot rivers, each 21 miles long, across the Great Level of the Fens.

The oldest surviving sluice at Denver was built in 1834 and is still in use, although its original wooden gates have been replaced with steel doors. Alongside is the new Great Denver Sluice opened in 1964. Together they perform several vital functions; they control the flow of the rivers and when necessary can divert floodwater into the Flood Relief Channel that runs parallel to the Great Ouse. They also serve as a lock gate between the tidal waters of the Ouse and the freshwater rivers to the south. Water diverted into the Cut-off Channel that forms a great loop through west Norfolk supplies drinking water as far south as Chelmsford and Colchester.

DIDLINGTON

This isolated hamlet eight miles south-west of Swaffham was once the centre of one of the largest and richest estates in Norfolk. Opposite the mediaeval church with its open, unpewed nave is the site of the former Didlington Hall. A tower and colonnade are the only remnants of a spectacular past in the Italian style.

There were several halls, but the last one was built in 1870, a huge mansion which was for many years the home of the Amherst family. All the buildings on the estate, the lodge, the bridges, the keepers' cottages, the laundry, the nursery, the garden, the school, the home farm and the stables date from the same period. In its prime the estate stretched from Oxborough to Buckenham Tofts, nearly ten miles across, and among those who came to shoot here was King Edward VII. The hall was demolished after the Second World War, during which it had been occupied by the Army.

The young Howard Carter, who went on to discover the tomb of Tutankhamun in 1922 (see also Swaffham entry), first came into contact with Egypt through the great collection at Didlington Hall: 'It is to Lord and Lady Amherst that I owe an immense debt of gratitude for their extreme kindness to me during my early career. It was the Amherst Egyptian collection, perhaps the largest and most interesting collection of its kind then in England, that aroused my longing for that country. It gave me an earnest desire to see Egypt', he wrote later.

Books from the Didlington library sold by Lord Amherst in 1909 raised over £57,000 and Caxtons bought en bloc privately before the sale realised £52,000, massive sums for that time. The bulk of Amherst's collection of Egyptian antiquities was auctioned at Sotheby's in 1921. Carter was closely involved with arrangements for the sale and prepared the detailed catalogue himself. Major European and American museums competed vigorously for the Amherst objects.

St Michael's church, set deep in wood and farmland, is still in use. The nave has been cleared of most of its fittings while the chancel, with marble altar rail, affords adequate seating for an adult population of around 20. Just over a century ago

Didlington had a population of 125 with a school built by Lord Amherst and work on the estate for everyone in the village who wanted it.

DILHAM

The North Walsham and Dilham Canal was always a modest affair, well in keeping with Dilham's reputation as a Broads backwater. The village between Stalham and North Walsham saw the canal open in 1826. It never became the success that was intended. The last wherry brought its cargo upstream from Bacton Wood staithe in 1934, and even in its heydey only three wherries a day could use the canal due to the water table.

Although the canal has long been abandoned, you can get along it in a small boat for about a mile if you can find the entrance. Many have voted it the most secluded and enchanting journey in Broadland, with water lilies brushing the side of the boat and branches meeting overhead. The less adventurous can settle for walks in the wooded glade along the canal's banks, where the lucky ambler may spot a kingfisher.

Dilham was the birthplace, in 1785, of one William Cubitt. A miller, cabinetmaker and millwright until 1812, he then became chief engineer at Ransome's works in Ipswich. He moved to London in 1823, and the Bute Docks at Cardiff, the South-Eastern Railway and Berlin waterworks were all constructed by him. Cubitt also invented the treadmill and was associated with the construction of Great Exhibition buildings in 1851, work that brought him a knighthood. Sir William was Lord Mayor of London in 1860.

The wherry was a distinctive Norfolk Broads sailing barge, with a single huge black sail. Before the First World War scores of these craft sailed the Broads. Over centuries they developed into perfect trading vessels for these waters, but fast and convenient transport by road and rail forced the wherries into decline. The last wherry to be built was the *Ella* at Coltishall in 1912. The Norfolk Wherry Trust was formed in 1949 to preserve for posterity an example of the local trading wherry – and the *Albion* sails to this day.

DISS

Built around a six-acre mere, this still-attractive town has the rare distinction of being lined up with two Poet Laureates. Generally considered to be the first to hold the post, John Skelton was Rector of Diss for 25 years, from 1504 until his death. Skelton Road in Diss is named after him. Sir John Betjeman, the most popular poet in this country since Kipling, voted Diss his favourite Norfolk town and was patron of the Diss Society. One of his poems describes a trip to Diss with Mary Wilson, wife of Sir Harold Wilson who had two spells as Prime Minister in the 1960s and 70s. Lady Wilson lived in the south Norfolk town as a child.

Before he moved to Norfolk, Skelton was tutor to Prince Henry – later Henry VIII – and claimed to have taught the prince to spell. Although he was a fine scholar, Skelton was also a scurrilous and vituperative rebel who took considerable delight in the crudeness of mediaeval life. This exposed itself most forcibly in his poetry which he often used as a deadly weapon to attack his enemies.

One of the best yarns concerns his keeping a concubine at Diss by whom he had several children. His parishioners complained and he was summoned to the Bishop's Palace in Norwich. He took with him two chickens as a gift. The Bishop was very angry from the first moment of their meeting. Skelton became just as enraged. Although he castigated him severely, the Bishop was still willing to accept Skelton's gift. The Rector of Diss said: 'My Lord, my capons have proper names. This capon is named Alpha – this is the first capon that I did ever give to you. And this capon is called Omega . . . and this is the last capon that ever I will give to you and so fare you well.'

For 138 years, from the time of the American War of Independence to the First World War, members of the Manning family were continuously Rectors of Diss. Their dates are: William Manning (1778), William Manning (1811), Charles Robertson Manning (1857) and Charles Upwood Manning (1899–1916).

DOCKING

One of Norfolk's unsung heroes was born in 1845 in this village that grew up in Saxon times on a crossroads leading to Fakenham, King's Lynn, Heacham and Hunstanton.

George Smith, youngest son of local shoemaker William Smith and his wife Frances, who came from nearby Ringstead, studied theology at St Augustine's College in Canterbury. He went to Natal as a missionary in 1871. When the Zulu War started seven years later he became attached to the British Army as a temporary chaplain and played a prominent part in the Defence of Rorke's Drift.

Although his heroics on that occasion evidently brought him the choice between a Victoria Cross and a permanent chaplaincy in the British Army, the makers of the film *Zulu* chose to ignore his efforts and wrote him completely out of the script! He got his permanent chaplaincy and went on to win further medals in Egypt before finishing his Army career at Preston where he died just after the Armistice had been declared in 1918.

Henry Rider Haggard, the great adventure writer who knew a heroic figure when he saw one, described George Smith as 'a big, red-bearded Norfolk giant'.

EAST DEREHAM

A straw poll in this ever-spreading town at the heart of Norfolk would reveal little about the man whose name is perpetuated by a row of thatched cottages alongside the parish church. Bishop Bonner's Cottage Museum, decorated with plaster pargeting, looks a treat. But even those who have made local history their specialist subject admit there is still an air of mystery about Edmund Bonner, Rector of Dereham from 1534 until 1540.

The illegitimate son of a priest, he was a rising young diplomat at the time. On several occasions while rector here he was sent abroad on missions connected with Henry's VIII's divorce from Catherine of Aragon. He had little time for parish work in Dereham, and it is not known how the cottages came to be

*Bishop Bonner's Cottage Museum near the parish church in
East Dereham.*

associated with him. They were built many years before he
became rector, probably in 1502. They may have been his
property or they could have been named in his honour when he
left to become Bishop of London in 1540, when he had not yet
earned the sinister title of 'Bloody Bonner'.

The notorious persecutor of Protestants in Mary Tudor's reign,
hounding over 100 to their death at the stake, he was portrayed
in Foxe's *Booke of Martyrs* as 'a monster in human form – whose
diabolical soul thirsted after the blood of those who thought not
as he did.' His tactics did earn him a rebuke from the Queen,
while his brutal manner and caustic tongue made him many

enemies. Indeed, he offended both the Pope and the King of France. For all that, in an age of religious doubt and conflict when many wavered or sought the safest course, he stood out clearly as one who had thought out his beliefs and defended them courageously.

Although in the early days of the Reformation he had accepted Henry VIII as head of the English church, when he discovered in the time of Edward VI that some reformers were determined to use this to impose a change of doctrine, he protested strongly and went to prison for his views. On Elizabeth's accession he refused the oath of supremacy and spent the last decade of his life in prison, stubbornly resisting all attempts to convert him.

East Lexham

A Yorkshireman of rare vision when it came to agriculture and conservation bought the East Lexham Estate in 1946. It looked a wreck after being ravaged by wartime activities. William John Foster went on to earn comparisons with Thomas William Coke, the great agricultural improver of the late 18th and early 19th centuries on the 50,000 acres of the Holkham Estate in the far north of the county. Foster's fieldwork in mid-Norfolk, a mile or so beyond Litcham, may have been on a smaller scale and carried out in vastly different circumstances – but rich Norfolk furrows had been followed.

When William Foster looked towards Lexham, the hall was empty and dilapidated, with shattered windows boarded up. The park was littered with Nissen huts. The place had been used as a military dump and an RAF bomber had crashed and exploded. Severe damage had been done to the woods by a team of Canadian loggers who cut out £15,000 worth of softwoods to meet the wartime need for timber. The course of the river Nar through the park and the village degenerated into a swamp. Houses in the little community were in a sad condition.

Invalided out of the Army after an attack of rheumatic fever in 1940, William Foster had given up his former ideas of a career in law and politics. As his business interests now lay partly in London and partly in Yorkshire, he and his wife thought they ought to live somewhere north-east of the capital. With nothing more specific than that to guide them, they started to explore East Anglia. They found Lexham on a snowy January day. Distinguished Norwich architect James Fletcher-Watson, a disciple of Sir Edwin Lutyens, was called in to restore the hall. Thousands of trees were planted and the village revived. It seemed only natural that Mr Foster should later be responsible for leasing nearby Litcham Common to the county council to become a nature reserve.

Of the village revival, Mr Foster said: 'We have always felt that it is not possible to get good men to work on a place where there are not good houses. This is not an original thought; Coke of Norfolk realised the truth of this matter a couple of hundred years ago.' Farming, forestry, drainage and landscape all took their turn in the spotlight before Mr Foster expressed the hope that his elder son and his successors would be able to 'carry on where we leave off'. Neil Foster has taken the family innings past the half-century mark in a corner of the county where constancy and continuity pay tribute to the far-seeing qualities of a modern improving landlord.

EAST WRETHAM HEATH

—— Just three miles north-east of the overspill town of Thetford, East Wretham Heath nature reserve weaves its strange magic. It features a variety of different habitats and encompasses two of Brecklands five natural meres – Langmere and Ringmere. These large ponds probably originated from small holes in the chalk which retained water and were gradually enlarged by solution. There are no apparent inlets or outlets to them, and they can vary from quite full to quite dry in a matter of a year or so.

Langmere, with its island, ancient Scots pines and wildlife, is more picturesque but Ringmere, with the unnatural regularity of its shape, the menacing darkness of its water and the vivid, delicate colours of its fringe, has mystery and beauty. In addition to heathland, the reserve also includes deciduous woodland of mature beech and hornbeam and a pine plantation dating from the time of the Napoleonic Wars. The heath is home to many insect species and butterflies are abundant. Grass snakes, adders, common lizards and great-crested and smooth newts are all present, as are toads which breed in large numbers in both meres. Wildfowl nest near the meres and some passage waders frequent the muddy shores. Crossbills have been seen in the pines and sparrowhawk and nightjar are recorded annually. Wheatears, stone curlews, stonechats, whinchats and great grey shrikes are occasional visitors to the reserve. Roe deer are resident. The reserve is open daily, and there is a nature trail for the physically handicapped, with guide ropes to help the blind and recorded commentaries along the way.

ECCLES-ON-SEA

—— This fascinating place situated almost exactly halfway between Cromer and Great Yarmouth long ago received the name of 'The Lost Village'. But not all has been lost, and after several days of fierce easterly winds and high seas during February 1986, parts were dramatically exposed on Eccles beach.

For the first time in many years scouring tides completely uncovered ancient foundations, roadways and sections of St Mary's church tower. More recently, further spectacular beach scours have revealed old walls, water wells, tracks, early pottery and even the gruesome remains of skeletons within St Mary's churchyard.

During mediaeval times, Eccles-Juxta-Mare consisted of about two thousand acres of land and was described as a 'good fishing town'. According to tradition much of the village was overwhelmed by the sea during the 17th century and the church, except for its tower, was left in ruins. Gradually advancing sandhills buried it with only its octagonal belfry protruding. Here it remained until the mid-19th century when high tides swept sections of the dunes away and left the tower standing isolated on the beach. Artists and photographers flocked to the spot.

Then, on 25th January 1895, the old round tower crashed to the beach into the teeth of a gale. Occasionally, throughout this century, storms have stripped the beach of sand, uncovering parts of the old church ruins. With almost every beach scour evidence has been revealed of the mediaeval village.

A large holiday bungalow estate was built by property developer Edward Bush as Eccles became a favourite haunt for people seeking the peace of unspoilt beaches. Only a small proportion of the planned 720 bungalows were ready before building stopped at the outbreak of the last war. Since then visitors and residents alike have received constant reminders of an ever-hungry North Sea. Major coastal defence studies and engineering works continue apace.

EDGEFIELD

'God moves in a mysterious way, His wonders to perform . . .' The opening lines of that stirring old hymn must carry extra meaning when the congregation strikes up in Edgefield parish church off the B1149 Saxthorpe-Holt road in north-east Norfolk. Canon Walter Herbert Marcon, Rector of St Peter and St Paul for a total of almost 63 years from 1875, moved the original church half a mile to its present position.

He was born in 1850 in Edgefield Rectory and died in the very same room in 1937. On taking up his post as father of the flock he found the church dilapidated and badly sited. The Black Death of 1349 had caused people to move away from around the church and the valley in which they lived. They settled on higher ground. Canon Marcon planned the exacting task of dismantling and reassembling the church in the centre of the village as it was then. Architect J. D. Sedding had surveyed the old church in 1876 and reported serious decay. He arranged the construction of the new building while Marcon raised the money needed. The rebuilding task took ten years, although the actual reconstruction lasted only two, from 1883–85. Marcon wrote: 'Bit by bit the roofs were taken down, the walls slowly razed to the ground – all the wrought stones were marked so as to ensure each stone going in its proper place.'

A new tower was built between 1907 and 1909 and in 1921 a First World War memorial clock was added as a tribute to the fallen. At the original site only the 13th-century octagonal tower is left standing in the Glaven valley. Nearby is an artificial mound built during the time of the Armada as a base for a warning beacon.

Marcon's father was Rector of Edgefield for 27 years before him, and a great uncle for 19 years before that. Prior to the Marcons taking over, Bransby Francis ministered in the tumbledown church for 63 years.

EGMERE

Once memorably described as 'not so much a hamlet, more a tasty little omelette', Egmere demands you to unscramble some of its evocative history. Sandwiched between the Creakes and the Walsinghams in the north of the county, this deserted village of one farm and a few cottages also boasts a bold beacon to the past, the ivy-clad ruin of the church of St Edmund.

Whichever way you approach you can spot the remains of the tower from a fair distance, the flints and mortars gleaming white and grey if the sun is out. The tower stands on a mound at the highest point of the whole site, most of it now under grass. From here the mounds and hollows of the former village can be plainly seen. To leave the road, climb over the gate and walk towards that tower is to walk into history.

Between 1553 and 1558 the parson, Thomas Hacker, complained to the Chancery Court in London that his predecessor had pulled down part of the church and taken lead from the roof. The lead and the biggest bell from the steeple had been sent to the coast for export. The church was finally desecrated by Sir Nicholas Bacon, Lord Keeper of the Seal under Elizabeth I, Lord of the Manor at Stiffkey and Francis Bacon's father. It was turned into a barn in 1602. (The Bacon-Egmere connection could also have inspired that 'omelette' line, perhaps?)

It seems that only a token Egmere could have survived the 16th century. *White's Norfolk Directory* of 1864 lists Egmere as having 56 inhabitants, but most of these must have lived in cottages near Egmere Farm and further along the road towards Walsingham. Some scholars claim it could have been a pre-

Roman village. Its roots may be obscure but there is no doubting the clear call of this peaceful but powerful spot just a short journey from the shrines and pilgrims of Walsingham.

FAKENHAM

The last remaining English example of the small horizontal retort, hand-fired gasworks has been preserved to attract visitors to a Norfolk town. Fakenham Museum of Gas and Local History on Hempton Road is open to the public during the summer months, showing the works as it existed just before closure in 1965.

Much of the works dates from before 1900, and the latest piece of equipment is the condenser, which bears the date 1953. In the late 1950s the economic advantages of the newer production methods led Eastern Gas to concentrate production, and all the small Norfolk works were linked to Norwich and closed. During this period maintenance was carried out on a short-term basis and several items of equipment at Fakenham were replaced by others transferred from works already shut. The purifier boxes came from North Walsham, the condenser from Thetford and the Livesey washer from Thetford, to which it had been moved from its original home at Brandon.

The manufacture of coal gas for public use began in this country with the formation of the London and Westminster Chartered Gas Light and Coke Company in 1813. It ended in the 1970s with the introduction of natural gas from the North Sea. The Fakenham works opened in 1846 and closed in 1965 when a trunk main was introduced to bring gas from Norwich. At its peak there were over 1,600 works in the country serving over 11 million customers and employing 125,000 people. Fakenham, one of the smallest works, served 500 customers and employed eight men.

On 21st November 1846, the *Norwich Mercury* reported: 'Fakenham has just been lighted by gas through the persevering and highly creditable exertions of Mr R. P. Spice, whose engagements as a gas engineer are of an extensive character. The works are an ornament to the town and the gas supplied of an unusual purity.'

In 1984 the Fakenham works was scheduled under Section I of the Ancient Monuments and Archaeological Areas Act, 1979, thus ensuring its preservation. Following intensive negotiations over several years the present arrangements were set up in 1986. British Gas has let the works on a full repairing lease for 125 years at a peppercorn rent to the Norfolk Historic Buildings Trust.

FERSFIELD

Norfolk historian Francis Blomefield (1705–1752) was a bold type when it came to working from home. Rector of Fersfield, near Diss, from 1729 until his death, he printed his *History of Norfolk* on his own press at Fersfield Rectory.

He got into deep financial trouble, partly because he was also a hunting man and kept his own pack of hounds. When he died at 47, halfway through the third volume of his history, he was so much in debt his executors would not act but handed over the administration of his estate to his two chief creditors. He died from smallpox caught on a visit to London – he had refused to be inoculated – and lies buried in the chancel of Fersfield church.

Blomefield started collecting material for his Norfolk history while he was still at school in Thetford, but it was not until he became rector of his home village that the work began to take shape. He sent out a comprehensive questionnaire to more than 200 people and travelled far and wide to collect and verify information. He had reached page 678 of the third volume when smallpox struck him down. His history of the county was completed by Charles Parkyn, Rector of Oxborough, near Swaffham.

It was through Francis Blomefield that the *Paston Letters* came to light. He was invited to Oxnead in 1735, and in the country house built by William Paston he found the precious letters, the earliest great collection of family letters in English, among the ancient tomes, document boxes and ledgers (see also Mautby and Oxnead entries).

FINCHAM

——— Still a constant source of reference and delight, Robert Forby's *Vocabulary of East Anglia* was compiled mainly while he was rector of this small parish on the main Swaffham-Downham Market road during the first part of the 19th century. Forby died in 1825, five years before the publication of his vital work on local dialect.

Born in Stoke Ferry, he went to school in King's Lynn and became a Fellow of Caius College, Cambridge. He then returned as a clergyman to his native county. He held livings in Horningtoft, Barton Bendish and Wereham before becoming Rector of Fincham in 1801, holding the post until his death.

His famous vocabulary, reprinted in more recent years, was 'an attempt to record the vulgar tongue of the twin sister counties, Norfolk and Suffolk, as it existed in the last twenty years of the 18th century, and still exists; with proof of its antiquity from etymology and authority.'

Forby supplemented his own knowledge with notes from numerous correspondents in other parts of Norfolk and of Suffolk and Essex. His vocabulary contained about two thousand words and phrases, and in a long and learned introduction he noticed some peculiarities which were not so much part of the dialect as of the local character and turn of phrase. Every compilation since has borne heavily on Forby's scholarship.

FORNCETT ST PETER

——— The Wordsworth saga has an intriguing Norfolk chapter set in a quiet corner of the Tas valley on a slight rise above the water meadows.

Here stands the church of Forncett St Peter and the handsome Queen Anne rectory to which the Rev William Cookson brought his new bride and young niece Dorothy Wordsworth in 1788.

Following the death of her mother, Dorothy had been brought up in Halifax where she met Jane Pollard, who was to remain a life-long friend. It is from the few surviving letters to her old

Forncett St Peter Rectory, with a Wordsworth connection.

schoolfriend that we learn something of Dorothy's time in Norfolk. On arrival she wrote to Jane: 'We are now happily settled at Forncett . . . my room is one of the pleasantest in the house. I wish you were here to share it with me. Some of the views are beautiful.'

Dorothy was soon involved in the life of the parish, visiting the sick and caring for her aunt's growing number of children. William Wilberforce, the man who did so much to get rid of slavery, was an old college friend of Mr Cookson and stayed on several occasions. He gave Dorothy an allowance of 10 guineas a year to distribute in what manner she thought best to the poor. She established a school for nine pupils at the rectory.

Although she was content with walks in the rectory grounds, her reading and letter writing, Dorothy sorely missed her brother William. He came only once to Forncett, for his six-week Christmas holiday in 1790 when Dorothy recalled: 'Every day as soon as we rose from dinner we used to pace the gravel walk in the garden till six o'clock when we received a summons (which was always unwelcome) to tea. Nothing but rain or snow prevented our taking this walk.' But the young poet found little favour with his uncle. Following the discovery that, while in France, he had met and fallen passionately in love with Marie Anne Vallon who bore his child, Dorothy stood loyally by her brother, but her relationship with her uncle deteriorated when William was refused any further invitations to Forncett.

Overcome with desire to see her brother again, Dorothy persuaded her uncle to let her travel to Halifax, a journey which proved to be her farewell to Forncett. Here she was reunited with her friend Jane Pollard and then soon after with William. The Cooksons remained at Forncett until 1804. The family connection with Norfolk was continued in the same year when Dorothy's brother Christopher became Rector of Ashby, near Loddon.

The church at Forncett remains very much as Dorothy and William must have known it, while the rectory has grown even more graceful with age. The water meadows are still a profusion of wild flowers in spring. They are now the only ancient meadows left in the Tas valley.

FOXLEY WOOD

—— The largest remaining area of ancient woodland in Norfolk, Foxley Wood covers about 300 acres and has stayed basically unaltered since the Domesday Book. Sadly, growing traffic demands took their toll of the village itself, the Norwich-Fakenham road cutting it in two. Foxley East calls to Foxley West . . .

Foxley Wood is well cared for by the Norfolk Naturalists'

Trust. In the past, trees such as hazel and small leaved lime were coppiced to provide poles for fuel and broom handles. It is hoped to re-establish the tradition.

A feature of the wood is a network of wide grassy rides, originally a help in the removal of timber and now supporting a variety of wild flowers including stitchwort, bugle or twisted hair-grass and food plants for several species of butterfly including meadow brown, comma, orange tip and white admiral. Goldfinch, sparrowhawk and greater and lesser spotted woodpeckers breed here.

The reserve is open from 10 am to 5 pm daily except Thursdays.

GATELEY

'This is one of those elusive villages which you expect to find quite easily by following the signposts – until you come to one which directs you back the way you have come. . .' So wrote a local newspaper reporter in February 1958 when he was sent to the tiny mid-Norfolk village to measure excitement over plans to build eight new semi-detached houses.

Well, Gateley remains small and easy to miss. The signposts can still play a trick or two. Dereham is nine miles away, Fakenham is seven and even the nearest village can only be reached by negotiating two miles of narrow by-roads. But the place has real charm with its few houses, a church which can only be reached via a farmyard, a hall nearly 250 years old and an overall sense of delight in its own isolation.

The village used to be big enough to support two cricket teams, but by the late 1950s only two or three players lived in Gateley with the rest of the line-up recruited from outside. Mr G. C. Hoare, who lived at Gateley Hall, brought his London staff down to play the annual fixture against the locals. Shades of 'England, Their England'.

In one remote corner of the parish at that time stood a cluster of cottages beside the common on a path which used to be known as Duck Walk. Older residents then could recall the village smithy, the little village school and the shop which sold sugar and vinegar. And they could remember when everyone living along Duck Walk had a flock of ducks or geese – hence its name. The small wooden Methodist chapel was built onto the side of the cottage. Gateley had no mains electricity, no mains water, no railway station and no bus service when the 'big development' was announced in 1958. It is a tribute to its gentle, unhurried ways that it has not buckled under to the sirens of progress like so many other small Norfolk communities.

GAYTON

Gleaming new cars rolling off the Mercedes production line carry a secret and unlikely passenger – a little piece of Norfolk. Flax grown in the county and at other sites across England is being used to make eco-friendly door panels for these luxury vehicles. And there are hopes that harnessing the oldest textile in the world to modern technology can breathe new life into a once-thriving industry.

Tucked away in a farm building on the edge of Gayton, a few miles from King's Lynn, is the largest and most modern industrial flax line in Europe. The £400,000 plant could be just the start of a new and expanding role for the 'golden yarn', named after the beautiful colour of the flax plant and because, in the ancient world, linen was the preserve of the wealthy.

Flax UK's premises are just a few miles from what remains of the flax processing factory at West Newton on the Sandringham Estate, a key player in the final chapters of the industry earlier this century. Flax production, which flourished during the 19th and early 20th centuries, declined and ultimately disappeared for a number of reasons. Cotton was growing in popularity and lent itself better to intensive farming and mechanised harvesting.

GIMINGHAM

An old jingle about a group of coastal villages still gets plenty of airings:

Gimingham, Trimingham, Knapton and Trunch,
Northrepps and Southrepps lie all in a bunch.

A useful little geography lesson, especially for visitors who stray from the bigger, better-known north Norfolk seaside resorts. Back in 1932, a special correspondent for the *London Evening News* claimed to have stumbled on 'what must surely be the strangest village in England.' He had arrived in Gimingham, notebook at the ready, and dutifully reported the following strange facts:

The village was without a baker, butcher, draper, tailor, fishmonger, bootmaker and resident policeman. According to parish records then available, at no time had any person bearing the name Brown, Smith, Jones or Robinson resided within its borders. There was no doctor, chemist or dentist, but there was one tiny shop and a railway – but no railway station. It had a public room but no pub. Moreover, it fronted onto the sea, although the sea was visible only in the far distance.

One farm owner was named Crowe and his predecessor was named Rookes. The churchwarden was a member of the Owles family, which lived next door to the Starling family. Mr White was the blacksmith, Mr Grey the carpenter while the schoolmistress was Green.

The London scribe also spotted 'a youthful old man' leaning on his gate 'intently watching my car as if it were the newest thing angels of sin had devised to invade rural peace.'

It was not reported if this missionary work came to be fully appreciated, although older residents claimed the capital correspondent might have found similar stories in other villages close by.

GLANDFORD

—— A model village far enough from the north Norfolk holiday rush to enjoy a rare brand of calm, Glandford stands as an attractive tribute to a truly benevolent squire. Sir Alfred Jodrell, who lived at nearby Bayfield Hall, rebuilt the parish church overlooking the Glaven valley and nearly the whole village as well.

Glandford Shell Museum.

He sent the local children to school in Holt a few miles away in
a covered wagon long before the education authorities thought
of such a scheme. He inherited the baronetcy in 1882 and grew
reluctant to leave the delectable Glaven valley. When he died in
1929, his body was placed in a coffin of plain oak without a
nameplate in accordance with his wishes.

The village consists of well-designed cottages with Flemish
gables, while a little building just north of the church contains a
collection of shells brought from every part of the world, and
other objects of interest including an embroidered panel by the
Sheringham fisherman-artist John Craske and a sugar bowl
Queen Elizabeth I used.

The shell museum is open to the public. It was built in 1915 to harmonise with the rest of the village. Work was carried out by men from the Bayfield Estate.

GODWICK

One of Norfolk's most compelling links with the past sits defiantly between the parishes of Tittleshall and Whissonsett. There are over 200 deserted villages in the county, but most sites have been destroyed by ploughing. The earthworks at Godwick are well preserved because the site is grazed by sheep and has never been disturbed.

It is one of the best surviving examples in the county and the only one open to the public. English Heritage has negotiated a management agreement with the landowner of Godwick to enable the site to be preserved and enjoyed by the public. Cars may be parked in the farmyard, and the site is open from 9.30 am to sunset between April and September. Keep dogs on a lead.

First settled in late Saxon times, Godwick was inhabited until the 17th century and remained a separate parish until the early 19th century when it was incorporated into the parish of Tittleshall. Following a run of bad harvests, the difficulty of cultivating the heavy boulder clay proved too much for the dwindling population.

The mediaeval village consisted of a sunken way running east to west with two other roads running off to the south. Along both sides of the street can be seen banks and ditches separating the tofts or individual house plots. Ruins of the church consist of a flint rubble base of the 13th-century tower which was raised as a brick and flint folly when the church was pulled down in the 17th century.

In 1585, in the middle of the village, Sir Edward Coke, Chief Justice and Attorney General to Elizabeth I, built a fine brick manor house. The ruins of the house were pulled down in 1962. The large barn was built over the line of the village street. It remains impressive, its west side decorated with blind pedimented and brick mullion and transom windows, never intended for use. The roof structure is original with alternating hammerbeam and queen strut trusses.

Sir Edward Coke established the family fortune. He was born at Burghwood Manor in the adjacent parish of Mileham. Together with his wife Bridget he is buried in Tittleshall church in the brick mausoleum with its remarkable series of monuments to the Coke family.

 ## GREAT FRANSHAM

The old Great Eastern Railway line from Dereham to King's Lynn closed in 1968 – but the wheels keep turning in colourful fashion at the Great Fransham halt.

When Bob and Ann Jenkins bought the derelict station house some years ago they planned to renovate it as a holiday home. But then they decided to enjoy their hobby of mending old engines and, on an occasional basis, making new machines. There's plenty of space to house their possessions in a garden which takes in part of the old station yard, a platform with a waiting room and which then stretches for a quarter of a mile along the old track.

A former British Telecom manager who took redundancy, Bob wanted a little business to go with a formidable display of historical transport ranging from old locomotives to a Victorian wheelchair. So he started producing penny-farthing cycles, selling them at 1,000 guineas apiece.

Bob went first to the Science Museum in London to draw plans from measurements of one on display. He was allowed in two hours before official admission time in order to study the bike at close quarters. 'They take a month each to construct, and I believe I'm the only manufacturer in Britain. I do stress that these are reproductions and I offer a Certificate of Unauthenticity with each one,' said Bob. He knew he was catering for a very limited market. If business were to get too brisk production would take up too much time and divert the Jenkins from their many other interests.

They have worked hard to retain the railway atmosphere of the buildings opened in 1847. Passers-by frequently call in to look round while Bob and Ann Jenkins are happy to show people their collection at leisure if an appointment is made.

—— While it is best known as a holiday playground, Yarmouth's wealth and prosperity were built on fishing, particularly the herring industry. Excavations in 1974 in the Fullers Hill area, regarded as the earliest part of the town, uncovered large numbers of fishhooks and fishbones, especially those of cod and herring, evidence of a community dependent on fishing as early as the 11th century.

The greatest expansion of the Yarmouth herring trade came in the 19th century when the coming of the railways enabled better and faster distribution and the building of the Fishwharf in 1869 improved landing and selling facilities. Yarmouth drifters began to fish further afield, heading north in the summer to fish off Northumberland and Yorkshire and returning for the home fishing in the autumn. In the winter, they might go south to catch mackerel off Cornwall or change their rig to go trawling in the North Sea.

Perhaps the biggest impetus to the Yarmouth scene was the increasing involvement of the Scots from the 1860s. Indeed, after 1885 there were generally more Scottish than home boats fishing from Yarmouth each autumn. Scots girls came by train in their thousands to salt and pickle herring in vast yards on the South Denes. Best years for the industry were just before the First World War, and 1913 broke all records when about a thousand vessels fished from Yarmouth catching and selling herring worth about a million pounds.

War put a stop to fishing as many drifters were taken into Admiralty service as minesweepers. The war and the Russian Revolution in 1917 severely damaged the Russian and German markets which never fully recovered. There was increasing competition between the wars and this, along with new fishing methods, began to decimate stocks. Overfishing brought gluts when record catches were sold at rock-bottom prices. There was no halting the decline although the Second World War did allow fish stocks to recover. They nose-dived again after the war and the cost of operating expensive vessels gradually made the industry unprofitable.

The Yarmouth fleet dwindled and the Scottish vessels came in fewer numbers. In the mid-1960s the last Yarmouth vessels were sold and Scottish vessels visited Yarmouth for the final time. Some herring curing firms, with their distinctive smoke houses, survive on the South Denes – but they now import herring from elsewhere.

GRESSENHALL

The old workhouse here at Gressenhall has been transformed into Norfolk's Rural Life Museum on the pretty outskirts of this expanding village. Another building to undergo a change of use was an old barn in the heart of Gressenhall, a few miles from East Dereham. This was converted to a Methodist chapel – and became widely known as 'God's Cottage'. The brick and clay lump building is attached to a very old cottage, or possibly a farmhouse. It is not certain which denomination originally used it as a place of worship, but it seems likely that this use dates from the early 19th century. By 1827 the Primitive Methodists were holding services here and the Fakenham Circuit, to which it belonged, stretched 20 miles to the north to include Cley on the coast. In later years it was placed on other circuits and the cause may even have lapsed for a while.

The Gressenhall congregation belonged to several Methodist Connexions until the 1932 amalgamation brought them into what is now the Methodist Church. In 1923 the building had been bought by the United Methodist Church after a house-to-house collection had raised part of the money and the owner had retiled the roof at his own expense.

Perhaps the most famous story from 'God's Cottage' tells how a preacher looked up from his sermon notes one warm summer afternoon to see three or four hens strut into the chapel. No-one wanted to eject them because of the commotion it might cause, and so they were allowed to file with dignity to the front. 'After gazing about them and clucking in approval, they settled down until the service was over.'

In the 1930s the Wesleyan cause at Barnham Broom, five miles from Wymondham, met in a room over the stables of a shop, and the sound of animals below would often be heard during the services. Barnham Broom chapel is now closed, but at New Holkham, near Wells, services are still held above cartsheds on the Holkham Estate in part of an old granary complex. Access is by outside stone steps and worshippers can look through windows at sheep and cattle on the park.

GUESTWICK

——— Perhaps it would be more appropriate to call this place 'Guesswork', for that is what many folk rely on to get there! Situated roughly between the small market town of Reepham and the large village of Foulsham, Guestwick ambles along quietly in a maze of narrow lanes twisting and turning as if they had been dropped from a snakes-and-ladders board.

Even if you have called before, you are still not sure where to find the points of arrival or departure. Another little road suddenly creeps up and, yes, more of the village awaits over there. The parish church lords over this quaint rural backwater. A good mile away, Guestwick Post Office and Stores provides a colourful riposte to the ever-quickening supermarket band-wagon. These homely premises, half hidden by a sprawling fir tree, used to be a horse-drawn tailor's shop on wheels plying its trade around Norfolk villages. Sheila Crick who has been minding this shop since 1961 said a lot of people still thought it was an old railway carriage as they pulled up to take photographs. 'That's probably because we are not far from the old railway station, and there aren't many people about who remember travelling tailors,' she added. She still has the iron wheels of this durable oddity built during the 19th century. Her late husband Fred used the premises for a radio and television repair business. 'He started in the days of accumulators,' said Sheila as she tidied boxes of vegetables outside. Personal service is guaranteed because there is room for only one customer at a time. An elderly local pensioner sang the shop's praises as he mounted his bike and headed for home down the lane.

HARLESTON

If you want to spark a lively debate, or even a good, old-fashioned argument in this busy little town between Diss and Bungay, just mention The Stone.

Situated in the alleyway connecting Broad Street with The Thoroughfare it retains a reputation for controversy. It is of glacial origin and one suggestion is that it arrived in its present position by natural deposition. Another theory is that the stone once stood outside a house called Haroldstone on the road to Needham. Then again, because the type of material from which the stone is made is usually found in Germany, it could have been brought overland or by boat down the river Waveney, which was once believed to have been navigable beyond Harleston. The top of the stone contains a cup-like hole. Some say rather fancifully it might have been used to catch human blood for sacrificial puposes when Saxon victims were beheaded. Others claim it was much more likely to have been used to disinfect money before use at the market during the Great Plague. The Harleston Stone is thought to have been used by Harold for his proclamations and by his herald to issue orders to troops defending strong points at Mendham, Homersfield and Shotford Bridge against enemies like Bigod of Bungay. It was also used for horse mounting. While it has no specific purpose today, anyone with brand new theories could well stand on it and expound loudly . . .

HAVERINGLAND

This scattered village nine miles north-west of Norwich is pronounced 'Haverland' by the locals. It might well have been rechristened 'Havenoland' when the last war broke out.

Haveringland Hall and surrounding parkland were taken over by the Air Ministry. Outlying farms and cottages were offered for sale, first to the tenants and then by public auction. A systematic blitz of the whole area was set in motion to make way for a fighter base known as the Swannington aerodrome.

Looking at the parish church of St Peter today, sentinel-like in the bare landscape, it seems remarkable that it once nestled in the shelter of great trees, oak, chestnut and beech. The approach to the church from the Norwich road led through massive wrought-iron gates as part of the lodge which housed the village post office, along a majestic avenue of horse chestnuts. A wall some miles in length encompassed it all.

All this was obliterated as the aerodrome took shape. A gap of about a mile was torn in the wall. The lodge gates were removed and the lodge itself blown up. As runways crossed and recrossed, each primrose hollow was destroyed by rubble brought by countless lorries from local gravel pits. Trees were felled and carted off in mournful procession. The hall survived for a time, useful for billeting flying men, but then it was demolished as well. Gaping cellars and a few outbuildings are all that remain of the great mansion built in the 1840s.

In June 1949 the *Eastern Daily Press* reported: 'The war brought the vast encroachment of a modern airfield which levelled the ground to each familiar landmark . . . a perimeter track replaced the wall that had encircled the estates . . . three years have passed and today all is still. Grass grows in runways. The Nissen huts stand gaping and derelict. The hall, which no man wants for a home, shorn as it is of its trees and gardens, is being demolished.'

Soon after the war ended, the hall was pulled down to make way for a caravan park. A Norfolk estate was a victim of war. But although the squires have gone at least the church continues to thrive.

Wooden stocks used in mediaeval times can be seen opposite the former King's Head pub, now a private residence. They have five leg-holes – hence the suggestion that Haveringland once housed a one-legged delinquent!

HEMPTON

—— Separated from Fakenham by the river Wensum, Hempton hangs on proudly to its own identity and its own history. From the priory established in the reign of Henry I to one of the biggest sheep fairs in England running until 1969, the village has followed a highly individual path over the centuries across its impressive green.

The founding of the priory had much to do with Hempton being on the road to Walsingham, the great pilgrimage centre of mediaeval England. The priory, very small and never rich, was included on the list of Norfolk's lesser monasteries drawn up in 1536 for immediate suppression. The monarch who gave the orders had, only a few years before, ridden past on his pilgrimage to Walsingham! The parish church of St Andrew on the Shereford road was abandoned and fell into ruin. Only the annual sheep fair in September, and two cattle fairs held annually until last century, broke the quiet daily life of the parish. It wasn't until the 19th century that Hempton was to make big news again.

The Rev Charles St Denys Moxon, assistant priest at Fakenham, lived in Hempton and he came up with the idea that the parish should have a church of its own once more. He obtained a grant of a piece of land on Hempton Green from the Lord of the Manor, the fourth Marquess Townshend, and at his own expense, aided by a few friends and a grant of £80 from the Incorporated Church Building Society, he built the Church of the Holy Trinity. This little building was intended to serve as the chancel of a larger church to be completed later. The present vicarage house was built in 1858, and the Church Room was used as a day school for many years.

By the 1950s it was clear the church was not big enough for the normal Sunday congregations, and it was decided to build an extension. The total cost, including payment for a new organ, was £4,700, and it was ready for consecration by October 1955. The Hempton Church Centenary Fund was supported with a rare will by the entire parish with fetes, concerts, dances and a gymkhana among the money-raising events. Over eight tons of newspapers were carried to the vicarage to be sold as waste paper, bringing in over £40.

Stones and dressed flints from the bombed church of St Michael at Thorn in Norwich were bought from the diocesan authorities. Also worked into the building were flints from the foundations of the old church of St Andrew in Hempton and stones from the ruined church of St Margaret at nearby Pudding Norton. Tiles and a bell from the disused church at Oxwick were given by the parishioners of Colkirk, and by one of the ironies of history, a gift was made of floor tiles from the ruined manor house of the Cliftons of Toftrees – the Clifton family having purchased the priory properties in 1572 and thus bearing some the responsibility for allowing St Andrew's church to fall into ruin by neglecting to provide a stipend for a vicar.

There were many other wonderful neighbourly acts – benches from Tittleshall and Raynham, a tabernacle from Ryburgh and a bookcase from Whissonsett among them. As Hempton celebrated on that memorable day in 1955, people flocked over the green from all directions to be sure of a place.

HETHEL

This small parish seven miles south-west of Norwich provided an important air base during the last war for the Americans. Since the early 1960s it has been the home of Lotus Cars. But the population has continued to dwindle to under 100 scattered across the village tucked away from the busy Wymondham-Bungay road. Its biggest claim to lasting fame is that it looks after Norfolk's smallest nature reserve – a single tree known as the Hethel Thorn. The enclosed reserve is in a meadow where horses and cattle graze near the parish church and covers a mere 140 square yards.

The Thorn is thought to be East Anglia's oldest living example of Crataegus nonogyna, and was also once known as the Witch of Hethel. The first Sir Thomas Beevor claimed to have a 13th-century document referring to it as a boundary tree, and it may also have been a meeting place during the insurrection of peasants when King John was on the throne. In 1864 the hawthorn was described as 'having a girth of 14ft 3in at 5ft from the ground, whilst the circumference of the space over which its branches spread is 31 yards.' Some of the trunk has died, but it clings to life. Certainly it is well over 700 years old and is now in the care of the Norfolk Naturalists' Trust, whose local members also tend the nearby churchyard of All Saints. You can hop over a stile to the meadow housing the thorn tree. Finding the site in the first place is a tricky business if you happen to venture far into the Hethel-East Carleton-Ketteringham triangle, but it is well worth the hunt.

Hethel Hall was demolished in the early 1950s. All that remains are the gardener's cottage, parts of the water garden and a clump of trees.

Hethel farmer James Rush of Potash Farm achieved national notoriety. On a dark November night in 1848 he put on an unconvincing disguise, made his way to nearby Stanfield Hall and there shot dead his landlord Isaac Jermy, the Recorder of Norwich, and his son. On 21st April 1849, about 12,000 people watched the last public execution to be held in Norwich as Rush went to the scaffold. His death mask is in Norwich Castle Museum.

If Hethel Thorn is the smallest nature reserve in Norfolk, Holkham, which embraces 10,000 acres of marsh, dune and mudflat along nine miles of coast, is the largest nature reserve in England. Thetford Forest Park, 80 square miles of largely conifer plantations, is the largest lowland forest in Britain.

HEYDON

'A little paradise gathered about a green', waxed Arthur Mee when he called here on the Norfolk leg of his national tour in the 1940s for the *King's England* series of books. Happily, Heydon's charm remains largely intact amidst woods and farmland four miles west of Aylsham.

Heydon Hall presides paternally over an idyllic scene used regularly by film-makers and television producers. Cottages clustered around the green and the impressive parish church give it an appealing bygone flavour. The handsome ornamental well on the green, a structure of red brick with terracotta dressings, was erected by Col W. E. G. Lytton Bullwer in 1887 to commemorate Queen Victoria's Golden Jubilee. Heydon Hall went up in the reign of Queen Elizabeth (1584). The Earle Arms pub is still a magnet for visitors and locals alike.

Heydon is far enough away from any other sizeable settlement to keep secrets of its own. The cameras will be back on a regular basis to use it as the yesteryear backcloth. Some claim that's all it can be, a pretty prop rather than a true community, but others insist it looks and feels like the old Norfolk.

A blacksmith's forge faces rows of neat homes, some with pediments, some with step gables, and all with pretty front gardens. An attractive estate village at the end of a cul-de-sac that leads to the hall – a lingering whiff of feudalism worth savouring.

HICKLING

—— Royal visits for wildfowling shoots have helped make Hickling Broad's history an illustrious one since it was purchased by a trio of sportsmen-naturalists in 1911. Haunt of the marsh harrier and bittern, and a place where in season you can still see the swallowtail butterfly, it is operated today by the Norfolk Naturalists' Trust. Hickling is the second oldest nature reserve in the country; only Wicken Fen in Cambridgeshire is older, by 12 years.

One of Hickling's most endearing personalities was Emma Turner, a pioneer of bird photography who carried out much of her work in Norfolk. She spent weeks at a time living aboard her houseboat *Water Rail* on Hickling Broad. The mooring point at the entrance to Heigham Corner is still known as Miss Turner's Island. As well as the houseboat, her fleet included the canoe *Ezekiel*, rowing boat *Merrythought* and sailing dinghy *Bittern*. She was awarded the Royal Photographic Society's Gold Medal for her work. One of Emma Turner's outstanding successes was photographing the first bitterns known to have been hatched in Norfolk after having been exterminated as a breed some 40 years previously.

She was one of the first women to be elected a Fellow of the Linnean Society and one of the first honorary women members of the British Ornithologists' Union. When Emma Turner died in 1940, the *Ibis*, journal of the British Ornithological Society, said: 'Though frequently alone in her houseboat on Hickling Broad, she never felt the loneliness ascribed to her by the Press. Her joy in nature by day and night was too vivid to admit of loneliness!'

To fully appreciate the beauty of this area today visitors can take the water trail, first of its kind in Britain. It was founded in 1970 when it won a special Duke of Edinburgh Countryside Award. The 440 acre broad is crossed twice, and highlight of the trail for most is a visit to the 60 foot high tree tower in Whiteslea Wood. The view is one of the finest in Broadland.

HILBOROUGH

Sitting astride the main road between Swaffham and Brandon, Hilborough yields few secrets to passing travellers. They see little more than some scattered farms and cottages and the ruins of St Margaret's Chapel, once a stopping place for pilgrims on their way to Walsingham. Perhaps there's a fleeting glimpse of the Georgian hall in the park overlooking the river Wissey. Before the Black Death the village was down the lane past the church to the east of the A1065, where the mill can still be seen.

Hilborough's main claim to fame is close association with two of the nation's principal heroes – Lord Nelson and the Duke of Wellington. During the 18th century the patronage of All Saints' church belonged to the Nelson family, and from 1734 until 1806 every rector was a Nelson, except for one who married a Nelson. The future Admiral's father was Rector of Hilborough before moving to Burnham Thorpe, where Horatio was born. Their first two children were born at Hilborough, and one of them was called Horatio; but both died in infancy and are buried in the sanctuary. Horatio, born two years after his father left Hilborough, visited the village many times to stay with his uncle, who had succeeded his father as rector, and his grandmother.

After the Battle of the Nile he was created a Baron and adopted the title Baron Nelson of the Nile and Hilborough in remembrance of his family's long association with the parish. Following his death at the Battle of Trafalgar in 1805 his brother William, Rector of Hilborough, presented the church with its famous Nelson chalice and patens which are used at festivals.

The Duke of Wellington lived at Hilborough Hall for a short

period after the estate was sold by the Caldwell family. The Caldwells had lived there for most of the 18th century and contributed a family vault on the north side of the chancel.

HILGAY

——— A great inventor never afforded the praise his vision and ingenuity deserved is buried in Hilgay churchyard. George William Manby died in his 90th year at Gorleston. He was born at Denver, close to Hilgay in west Norfolk, and educated in Downham Market.

Manby bought the Wood Hall Estate in Hilgay in 1804 and clearly had deep affection for the village. He became a churchwarden and his name is inscribed with that of his fellow chuchwarden J. Portler on Hilgay church tower which was built in 1794. There is a tablet in Hilgay church eulogising his father, Matthew Pepper Manby. It was placed there by George, who described himself as 'the last remaining branch of a long line of ancestry and the last of that name.'

George Manby invented the rocket lifesaving apparatus as well as a chemical fire extinguisher, elastic sheets for use at fires, harpoons for whaling, improved types of lifeboats, howitzers and dredgers. There is an impressive exhibition of his inventions in the Great Yarmouth Maritime Museum.

A tablet on the back of his Gorleston home in High Road reads: 'In commemoration of the 12 February, 1808, on which day directly eastwards of the site the first life was saved from shipwreck by means of rope attached to a shot fired from a mortar over the stranded vessel, a method now universally adopted and to which at least 1000 sailors of various nations owe their lives – 1848'.

He often complained about the government's indifference to his inventions, and thought Queen Victoria should have given him a knighthood. In 1803 Manby went to London to offer his services to the Secretary of War to assassinate Napoleon. He was refused – and instead he was appointed Barracks Master at Great Yarmouth. It was here that he witnessed a shipwreck involving the loss of 200 lives, a disaster that impelled him to develop the idea of a mortar and rocket apparatus for throwing a line from shore to ship.

HINGHAM

For those who think twinning is a comparatively new trend, the neat little market town of Hingham provides a stirring story of long-established links across the Atlantic.

In the early 17th century a number of folk from this settlement a few miles west of Wymondham chose the uncertain future of a new life in America where they founded the colony of Bare Cove – now renamed Hingham – in the state of Massachusetts. In 1637, these early settlers were joined by another local boy, Samuel Lincoln, great-great-great-great-grandfather of Abraham Lincoln who became the 16th President of the USA in 1860.

Samuel was a 15-year-old apprenticed to Francis Lawes, weaver and mariner of Norwich, when he set sail for America with Lawes and his family.

Ties between the two Hinghams were strengthened in the early part of this century. A bronze bust of Abraham Lincoln was unveiled in the Norfolk church by the American Ambassador in October 1919. 'Chips off the old block' had been colourfully remembered a few years before. In 1911, Hingham in Norfolk sent an ancient mounting block to their New England friends. A couple of years later, Hingham in Massachusetts acknowledged the gift in kind by sending back the granite boulder which stands today outside the post office opposite the historic White Hart Inn.

The first Lincoln Hall in one of Norfolk's best looking communities – it has been likened to a set for a Jane Austen novel – was an old army hut transported from near Thetford behind a traction engine. The present hall was built alongside the original meeting place and opened in 1977.

HOE

One of only two Norfolk villages with as few as three letters – Oby, ten miles north-west of Yarmouth is the other – Hoe offers extremes a few miles from Dereham. There is a highly mechanised fruit and vegetable farm at Gorgate Hall, where I suffered backache and boredom as a lad trying to earn a few bob in the holidays. In contrast there's Hoe Rough, owned by the Norfolk Naturalists' Trust and opened by colourful countryside campaigner David Bellamy in 1989.

The reserve covers 25 acres and is situated in the valley of a river Wensum tributary. One part of Hoe Common, this site supports a diversity of habitats including one of the finest remains of unimproved grasslands in Norfolk, woodland, mossy heath, anthills and a pond. Derelict buildings are the remains of pig houses from the days when pigs were allowed to forage.

HOLME HALE

Parts of the old Nag's Head date back to 1140, making it one of the oldest houses in Norfolk. Built of clay and with a thatched roof, it originally resembled a barn. There was no glass in the windows, space being filled with hazel sticks. There was no chimney either, just a hole in the roof for the smoke to escape through. Standing so close to the church in this village five miles from Swaffham, its early use could have been as a rectory, brewing church beer, the start of its life as a local inn.

Village chronicler Alec Hunt recalled how the pub got its name. A bishop stayed at the house in 1347 and while he was there his favourite horse died. The old gentleman was grief-stricken and he extended his visit by a week. Legend has it that from that day onwards the inn became known as the Nag's Head. Three cottages were built opposite at the time and, strange to report, when they were demolished in 1969 a horse's head was found in a clay lump.

Many a society to help the poor was formed in the local pub. At the Nag's Head one such club collected money to maintain a house in Church Lane so no family would have to leave the parish in the event of a farmer turning them out of a tied cottage.

The railway reached Holme Hale in 1875, forging new links with other communities. Milk was sent to London on the early morning train, the milk arriving at the station in tall churns holding about 16 gallons. The station was nicknamed 'The Aviary', because the three porters working there were called Bird, Sparrow and Eagle! The latter lived at neighbouring North

Pickenham and was very fond of his bed. The driver of the 6.10 am train from Swaffham would blow his whistle to wake Fred Eagle up, open the gates himself and leave them for Fred to close when he arrived for work on his cycle.

HOLT

Gresham's School, whose old boys include poet W.H. Auden, musical maestro Benjamin Britten and broadcasting pioneer John Reith, has contributed much to the prosperity and development of the town of Holt.

The Gresham family originated from the nearby village of the same name, moving into the Manor House in Holt in the 15th century. Sir John Gresham, one-time financial agent of Cardinal Wolsey and Thomas Cromwell, was Lord Mayor, Sheriff and Alderman of the City of London and member of the Mercers' Company. He gained plenty from the redistribution of monastic lands and, after deciding to found a school, bought the Peres Manor House – 'a substantial and commodious property' – for his brother William.

With the Mercers' Company already having its own school, Sir John signed over the building to the Worshipful Company of Fishmongers, of which he was a member, in 1554 with two manors, various pieces of land in Norfolk and freehold property in Cripplegate in London. Sadly, he died of plague a week later. The school officially opened in 1562 to provide education for 30 free scholars plus boarders and day-boys.

All the early headmasters were practising clergymen, although this did not automatically spell high standards on their part. Thus Rev Thomas Cooper, Rector of Little Barningham and appointed Usher to the school, was dismissed in 1632 for non-attendance and later hanged on Christmas Day in Norwich for his part in the Royalist rebellion of 1650. Henry Mazey (1660–65), later to become headmaster of Norwich Grammar School, was clearly a disciplinarian for in later years the Norwich boys petitioned the Mayor of the city asking for his removal. The Rev Thomas Atkins (1787–1809) was dismissed and the Rev Benjamin Pullan (1809–58), Vicar of Weybourne, taught boys by repetition and beat them if they got it wrong. One of the last of the old order was Charles Elton, a savage disciplinarian who beat the boys unmercifully. He resigned in 1867.

HORSHAM ST FAITH

Paintings from the past light up an intriguing part of this Norwich suburb, fighting with determination to retain something of the atmosphere of a village north of the city's airport. Ruins of the original Benedictine Priory of St Faith, founded in 1105, survive at Abbey Farm next to the church.

Recent restoration work in the farmhouse uncovered an outstanding series of 13th-century wall paintings in what was once the refectory. They illustrate the life of Robert Fitzwalter who, according to legend, was imprisoned while returning from a pilgrimage to Rome. After praying to St Faith he was miraculously rescued and founded the priory in gratitude.

The upper half of the wall paintings was discovered in 1924. The lower part was not investigated as it was covered in oak panelling. This meant the descriptive paintings of the foundation of the priory remained hidden and unknown. In 1958 the then owner sold Abbey Farm to a rose-growing concern, but the farmhouse was left empty, became neglected, vandalised and open to the elements. The Ministry of Works boarded up the windows and doors. Then in 1968 it was sold to Robert Newell of the University of East Anglia. He was responsible for bringing all the wall paintings to light. The upper floor was removed and replaced by a gallery so the whole wall could be viewed in its original state. Mr Newell also fully restored and repaired the abbey buildings and created a fine garden as a suitable setting.

HOUGHTON-ON-THE-HILL

The church of St Mary the Virgin and a farmhouse nearby are all that remain of this old farming village between Watton and Swaffham. Located on the South Pickenham Estate,

Houghton-on-the-Hill has a proud history which included Roman occupation. But the village began to vanish in the late 1800s when families employed on the big farms lost their jobs and drifted towards major urban centres.

The village became empty and silent, prompting the estate to pull it down. The church, place of worship since 1090, fell into disrepair, its roof tattered, religious icons damaged and its tower smothered by ivy which hid its very existence down a muddy track. Now, after years of painstaking restoration work at St Mary the Virgin, there are big hopes of a Houghton revival led by historian Bob Davey.

Formerly from Sussex, he fell in love with the church after his wife took him to the building she spotted while on a rambling tour. The love affair which began in 1992 has led to the recovery of precious paintings hidden behind plaster on the church's inside walls. They include Romanesque wall paintings described as the most important to be discovered in 20 years. A fund-raising drive was launched to save and restore the paintings inside the Grade I listed church. Supporters have also been working towards the complete restoration of the two-storey bell tower. Cracked in 1916 by a German bomb, the tower contains a tiny two-chair chapel which has become a spiritual retreat for hundreds of visitors. A feasibility study has been backed to turn the redundant village into a new centre for cultural and artistic development.

There is, however, a sinister side to the Houghton revival hopes. St Mary the Virgin became a haven for devil worshippers in the 1960s, and the pagan inverted crosses scrolled into its walls are still visible. Pagans headed to the church because it was never deconsecrated after being abandoned in 1937. After the devil worshippers were moved out a cleansing ceremony was conducted to rid St Mary's of the evil influences which had haunted its sanctified walls for almost 30 years.

HOW HILL

This educational centre, with courses for adults as well as classes for children, glories in the most delightful of

Broadland settings. The big thatched house is an ideal place from which to soak up some of Norfolk's most precious environment amid the marshland and reedbeds. Following the signs from Ludham and entering the car park just before the windmill, you'll find an impressive oak tree – presented by Adolf Hitler.

So what is the connection between an evil dictator and this gem of a wildlife location? Well, the Boardman family, who originally owned the property, had a keen sailor in young Christopher. He had an early Navy career after spending much of his childhood sailing on the Broads. In 1934 he attempted to win the America's Cup for England in his yacht *Endeavour II*. Seeking more excitement a couple of years later he took *Lalange* to Nazi Germany to compete in the Berlin Olympics, overseen by Hitler himself.

Competing with eleven other nations, Boardman and his colleagues won the gold medal for Britain. As part of the Olympic ceremony Hitler awarded each winner an oak sapling. On 20th September 1936, Norfolk's sapling was duly planted at How Hill. With a plaque explaining its background it has flourished and grown – but the gold medal turned out to have been made almost entirely of base metal!

HUNSTANTON

—— A memorial plaque in the Esplanade Gardens gives the names of 31 people who lost their lives in the 1953 east coast floods. Fifteen of the victims were British and the other 16 were citizens of the United States. An American serviceman Reis Leming saved 27 people from drowning and was awarded the George Medal. 'Shucks, it wasn't much', was the statement by the modest hero who returned to the town 40 years later.

It was a dark and devil-driven night, Saturday, 31st January, when a combination of an exceptional high tide and freak storm conditions at sea produced an unstoppable surge which rendered man's existing sea defences virtually useless. A train leaving Hunstanton just before 7.30 pm was halted in its tracks before reaching Heacham. The floodwater was capable of putting out the engine's fire. Huts and bungalows were washed from the beach areas and about 50 of these disappeared or were demolished. Local folk worked in terrifying conditions to help rescue trapped tenants and bungalow owners along the South Beach.

American servicemen from the Sculthorpe camp were drafted in with equipment and machines never seen in the town before. Leading the way was non-swimmer Corporal Leming who rescued trapped people by wading up to his neck in treacherous waters and, pushing a dinghy, went from rooftop to rooftop taking off the 'sitting ducks'. He was in the water from 8.45 pm until 4.45 am when he collapsed from exposure and slipped into unconsciousness.

For East Anglia it was the most catastrophic tragedy in modern history. There were almost 100 deaths in Norfolk and Suffolk while thousands of people were driven from their homes. More than 1,400 sites from Lincolnshire to Kent were breached, and in all 307 people were drowned.

INGOLDISTHORPE

——— Close to Sandringham and the sea, this lively parish is pronounced 'Inglesthorpe' – but the extraction of the gold ought not to take the shine off a highly individual village sign. It guards the entrance to the recreation field and depicts two famous local ladies, the benefactress and the formidable dame.

On the left, Eleanor Coates Tylden, Lady of the Manor until her death in 1928, on the right, Agnes Bigge in Quaker dress. She died in 1608. Ingoldisthorpe's own Women's Institute was not formed until 1975, and so it was the combined group of Snettisham and Ingoldisthorpe who commissioned Harry Carter of Swaffham to make the sign for presentation to the village in 1968.

Mrs Tylden became Lady of the Manor in 1909, teaching at the Sunday school, training the Choral Society and building the church hall. 'As I drive around in my horse and chaise, the villagers show great respect. When I visit their homes, I suggest ways of rearranging their furniture to improve the room.' She counted Queen Alexandra among her friends. 'She calls on me at the Manor whenever she stays at Sandringham House. On my 100th birthday, January 31st, 1923, I was honoured by the visit of five Queens and one Empress – Queen Alexandra, Queen Mary, the Queens of Norway, Spain and Rumania and the Dowager Empress of Russia.' The Manor, converted into a hotel and country club, was destroyed by fire in 1982.

Mrs Bigge was the wife of Thomas Bigge and the daughter of Thomas Rogerson, rector of the church in the 1500s. When she died she left £5 towards repairing the church and the then considerable sum of £10 to be invested in the care of the rector. She directed that the profits were to be distributed annually on St Thomas' Day, July 3rd, 'unto the most aged and needy poor of this parish.' Three pieces of land totalling three acres were bought with the bequest. By 1833 the income was enough to buy coal at 14s 6d for two families and to provide 15 others with four or five shillings each.

In 1896 the Charity Commissioners decided that the parish council should appoint two trustees to administer the charity with the rector, a practice that continues to this day. Some of the land was sold in 1933 for £50, which was reinvested. Nowadays at Christmastime a number of Ingoldisthorpe residents aged 90 have reason to thank Agnes Bigge for her benevolence.

IRSTEAD

A little corner of broadland nestling in the marshes of the river Ant, Irstead has escaped the development excesses rife among its bigger neighbours. Smart, detached houses look across acres of open farmland on the edge of watercourses and broads while the road to the 14th-century thatched church duly delivers its promise of charm and serenity.

Many visitors arrive by boat and moor up at Irstead Staithe, some of them remembering when there were six big lime trees in the churchyard. One fell victim to the hurricane of October 1987, just missing the church when it toppled.

Near the east window is the grave of Sir Francis Palgrave (1788–1861). He was founder of the Public Record Office and

First Deputy Keeper. His son, Francis Turner Palgrave, earned fame as editor of *The Golden Treasury* of lyrical poetry.

ISLINGTON

Despite being 'taken over' by bigger neighbour Tilney St Lawrence and labelled 'Tilney cum Islington', a fiercely independent spirit has asserted itself just over four miles south-west of King's Lynn. Islington insists it is a separate parish, and has a village sign to aid the cause. It depicts a young lady sitting on a grassy bank – and therein lies another controversy.

The bailiff's daughter of Islington is remembered through the touching 15th-century ballad of that name. It begins:

> There was a youth, and a well-beloved youth,
> And he was the squire's son;
> He loved the bailiff's daughter dear
> That lived in Islington.

The ballad goes on to tell how, to obstruct the path of true love, the squire sent his son to London Town. But true love did triumph in the end. There has been much argument over the years concerning the Islington referred to in the old song. Islington in London put in strong claims, but shrewd judges suggested any man intending to thwart the course of true love would interpose a far greater distance than the matter of a few miles which at one time separated the old London Islington and London Town.

There are no doubts in the Norfolk parish that their claims are fully valid. Fred Ham, who designed the village sign, reckoned arguments arose largely due to the confusion of two ballads of about the same date – The Bailiff's Daughter of Islington and The Fair Maid of Islington. 'The latter refers to the immoral means by which the maid earned her living and is surely more in keeping with the great metropolis than a very small and quiet country village', said Fred.

Independent Islington rests its case on a grassy bank.

KETTERINGHAM

A small settlement holding on bravely to its rural soul amid a sea of roads, increasing traffic, supermarkets and concrete, Ketteringham was responsible for scandalising Norfolk society in the 1780s. Six miles south-west of Norwich, Ketteringham Hall, a large Tudor mansion set in a pretty park beside a lake, was the centre of a remarkable story starring a female Scarlet Pimpernel.

A memorial is on the north wall of the nave of Ketteringham church to Charlotte Atkyns, a beautiful Irish actress whose dancing and singing took her to the top of the bill at Drury Lane. Charlotte Walpole married Edward Atkyns, wealthy young squire of Ketteringham, in 1780. Norfolk society felt the actress was hardly respectable with all her glamour and extravagance. She was cold-shouldered on her visits to Norfolk and the pair were always glad to return to the warmth and gaiety of the West End. They travelled on the Continent where Charlotte struck up a close friendship with the Queen of France, Marie Antoinette. When the Revolution came and the Queen was imprisoned and condemned to death, Charlotte tried to help her escape. She disguised herself in scarlet coat, breeches and three-cornered hat to gain an interview. But that was as far as this Scarlet Pimpernel got. After her husband's death – and he had been a strong restraining influence on her adventurous streak – Charlotte spent a lot of money on wild schemes to rescue the little Dauphin. Again, she failed.

Her last years were spent in comparative poverty simply because she had helped so many others financially. The actress, who even dressed up as a soldier of the National Guard in an effort to rescue the Queen she so admired, died in Paris and lies in an unknown grave.

KING'S LYNN

It took over 350 years for John Mason's home town of King's Lynn to start appreciating his achievements. Mason (1586–1635) founded the state of New Hampshire in the USA, was an adventurer, colonial governor, merchant, army paymaster, entrepreneur – and even a pirate.

He left a large American estate to Lynn, but no-one in the town of modern times knew anything about him and he was omitted from all of Lynn's most important histories. Nor was there a single mention of him in the town's museum or library. Then his links with Lynn were confirmed in 1991 from the register of births of St Margaret's church held in the Norfolk Records Office in Norwich.

In New Hampshire, the state Captain Mason founded, there has long been keen interest, especially with regard to the long and painful controversy over his will. When he died in 1635 Mason left huge stretches of American land to his close relatives and to the town of King's Lynn. He bequeathed to Lynn an estate of some 2,000 acres for the rent of one penny a year. He also required that within five years of his death the town should send five families to New Hampshire to settle the land. Profit of the settlement was to be distributed to the town's poor.

Generous offers, but the town corporation was worried about the cost involved in sending out five families. It was decided the town did not want to undertake such a venture, and it went on to give the estate away to one Robert Greene of Swaffham in 1654.

Among other achievements Captain Mason was Governor of Newfoundland, Deputy Governor of New England and Paymaster of the British Army. He was convicted as a pirate early in his career, and James I's favourite, the Duke of Buckingham, was murdered in Mason's Portsmouth home. Son of a King's Lynn merchant, John Mason is buried in Westminster Abbey.

LANGHAM

—— The Langham Dome continues to inspire weird and wonderful guesses as to what it was built for on this village airfield near the north Norfolk coast over half a century ago.

Along with the old control tower, converted into an office and stores, it is the only obvious survivor from the buildings which saw over 2,000 service personnel stationed at Langham in 1945. The airfield was sold in 1961, mainly returning to agricultural use and with turkey-rearing sheds built on part of the concrete areas. So, what was this remnant looking like an upturned Norfolk dumpling used for? It was an anti-aircraft training dome, almost certainly constructed in 1943 during the time the airfield was closed for rebuilding, and probably in use for only just over a year.

Originally, 25 of these dome trainers were planned across the United Kingdom, but in the end 40 were constructed, 25 feet high and with a 40 foot internal diameter. Appropriate film was projected onto the inside of the dome and trainee gunners practised dry firing at images on the film. Lighting and sound were available to make the exercise more realistic. The dome at Langham may have been the only one to go up in Norfolk. It is certainly the only one left.

LETHERINGSETT

—— Johnson Jex, blacksmith and horologist, rests in the churchyard of this small village crouching beside the main road a mile out of Holt. He 'advanced from the forge to the crucible, and from the horseshoe to the chronometer, acquiring by mental labour and philosophic research, a vast and varied amount of mechanical skill and general knowledge.' These are among lines on his tombstone, lines inscribed in the shape of an anvil. He died in January 1852.

Johnson Jex was the son of a blacksmith at Billingford, about 15 miles away in the middle of Norfolk. At a very early age he made valuable improvements to agricultural machinery. He also showed a keen interest in clock and watchmaking, often playing truant from school to help in a local watchmaker's shop.

He arrived in Letheringsett at the beginning of the 19th century and set up a foundry in the back premises of a house on the Blakeney road still known as the Foundry House. As well as continuing his experiments with agricultural machinery, he achieved considerable success with a thermostatically-controlled greenhouse of his own design. But his main interest was in horology. At over 60 he taught himself the French language in order to study French horological works and he made valuable contributions to the art of watchmaking. All the tools required he made himself, and on the watchplate of one of his watches he engraved these lines:

> I, Johnson Jex, a blacksmith bred,
> With some strange crankums in my head
> And tools on which I could depend
> By me invented. For a friend
> This time-piece made from end to end.
> If this your mind it should perplex
> Behold my name, 'tis Johnson Jex.

Watches, a lathe and other tools Jex made are in Norwich Castle Museum.

LITCHAM

An old coach barn, a Grade II listed building, houses a growing collection of country bygones collected by Litcham Historical and Amenity Society. The village museum was opened in 1992 and immediately won a Rural Villages Ventures competition. It is also the home of Ron and Brenda Shaw, and their interests do not end with trying to find space for all the museum items. In the extensive grounds of Fourways an underground lime kiln was discovered in 1958 and restored. It closed down at the turn of this century after 200 years of life. It is also now a Grade II listed building. The old workings, covering over three acres behind the museum, can still be seen, although the area is a self-set woodland and registered bird sanctuary. Mrs Shaw has been looking after injured birds for over 30 years, releasing them back into the wild when they have recovered. She has been a member of the RSPCA for 60 years and has been honoured by the RSPB for her work.

The Shaws' home was originally a tollhouse, probably built in the 18th century. The last toll collected was fourpence for a horse-drawn vehicle in 1913. Before museum artefacts moved in, the old coach barn was used as a stores and electrical workshop. Litcham village museum is open 2pm to 5pm on Saturday and

Sunday afternoons from April to October. Entry is free, but donations are welcome.

LITTLE WALSINGHAM

—— A vision which fired the mediaeval mind still continues to draw hundreds of thousands of pilgrims each year to 'England's Nazareth', the Shrine of Our Lady at Walsingham. This is Little Walsingham, planned and built to cater principally for pilgrims. Ironically, Great Walsingham nearby marks a swift return to the more traditional peaceful village life of Norfolk. Although Methodists are very much in the minority in Little Walsingham, they have good cause to reflect with pride on achievements over the years. The exterior of the Methodist church was built in 1793–94, making it the oldest still in use in East Anglia. It is a four-square brick building with arched windows and pillared portico. The tiled pyramid roof is topped by a weather-vane. The interior is in the plain style of 18th-century Methodist preaching houses. The gallery is on three sides and still has the original pews.

John Wesley, founder of Methodism and great travelling preacher, visited Little Walsingham on Tuesday, 30th October 1781. He wrote in his journal: 'At two in the afternoon I preached at Walsingham, a place famous for many generations. Afterwards I walked over what is left of the famous Abbey, the east end of which is still standing. We then went to the Friary, the cloister and chapel whereof are most entire. Had there been a grain of virtue or public spirit in Henry VIII, these noble buildings need not have run to ruin.'

Early documents are still kept in the Methodist church. Copies of licences which gave worshippers legal protection as Dissenters from the Church of England can be seen. One for Great Walsingham is dated 1791 and the other for Little Walsingham dated 1794. The Methodist church, which underwent a big renovation programme in the 1980s, stands close to the main street and in sight of pilgrims as they process. Many seek to enter as it is customary for pilgrims to visit all 'holy houses' while in Walsingham. The Methodists share in various events arranged during the Week of Prayer for Christian Unity.

LYNG

A pretty village on the river Wensum, seven miles north-east of Dereham, Lyng has more dark secrets than most. Headless horses, a bleeding boulder, an ivy-covered ruin and buried treasure all conspire to make moonless nights a real test of nerve for rural wanderers.

It was once a regular custom to let the schoolchildren of Lyng Easthaugh, a hamlet a mile from the village, go home early on winter afternoons. The King's Grove was the cause of all the concern. The King whom local tradition credited with a Lyng connection was King Edmund the martyred saint, King of the Angles, who it is said fought a battle here against the Danes. If this was the scene of the battle, the dead would have been strewn all along the Grove.

Then there came strange boulders, the largest one reputed to bleed on certain nights. A local parson suggested the boulder had gathered grisly legends around it because originally it had an important role as an altar-stone on which animals or even human sacrifices were offered. . .

Another story said that there was treasure under the stone and that there had been various efforts to recover it. The ivy-covered ruin of a nunnery added to the macabre picture. In the 19th century several skeletons were found between the old nunnery, St Edmund's Chapel, and the Grove. A potent local legend tells of a silver chalice being found in a drain, possibly the old river course, near the chapel. The workmen who found it argued fiercely. When one uttered a dreadful oath the chalice jumped back into the stream and was lost.

Perhaps Lyng and the immediate area around make a perfect case for extra street lighting. Then again, some of those blood-curdling yarns could be clever ploys to stop the village expanding too much!

MARSHAM

From crow-scaring to Westminster, the story behind the champion of farmworkers in Norfolk is as durable as it is stirring. George Edwards began his working life frightening birds on the land. He went on to become an MP, knight, preacher, alderman, magistrate and founder of a major union.

He was born in abject poverty at Marsham, near Aylsham, in 1850. The union he founded unveiled a plaque at his birthplace, Meadow View, 2, Fengate, 140 years later. Ironically this honour came as the birthplace of the original union at North Walsham was razed to the ground by developers. The Angel Hotel, where George held his inaugural meeting in 1906, was demolished to make way for flats.

He is also remembered at Fakenham where he later made his home and died. He is buried in the town cemetery where an annual service and wreath-laying at his memorial is held. His connections with the town are represented on the town sign by a plough.

George could not read or write when he married and his wife, Charlotte, became his teacher. When the first union collapsed he went lecturing and then turned his back on the land. But pressure from the men he had so inspired persuaded him to have another go. In 1906 the Eastern Counties Agricultural Labourers' and Smallholders' Union was born. He regained his county council seat and tasted success after a six-month strike at Trunch. However, a long and bitter dispute in the St Faith district near Norwich led to a split in the union, and it was out of this reorganisation that the national union grew.

In 1923 the great strike of 10,000 workers took centre stage when farmers tried to reduce pay and to lengthen hours. George Edwards became a national figure. He received the OBE, entered Parliament representing South Norfolk for Labour at the age of 70 and was knighted in 1930.

He travelled a long way from that cottage in Marsham, but never forsook the common touch in his pioneering work for rural trade unionism.

MARTHAM

—— Law and order in rural areas is a constant subject for lively debate, with regular complaints about resources being on the thin side. Well, the village of Martham, ten miles from

Yarmouth, took the matter most seriously – with the church playing an influential role.

For as far back as church records go it seems Martham had two and sometimes three constables appointed at the annual vestry meetings. They had to be educated people, able to read and write and keep records. One constable was for Highgate, the central part of the village around the green, one for the area known as Cess and one for Damgate. Their duties were to maintain law and order, to take offenders to appear before the magistrates and, after the 1662 Act of Settlement, to escort paupers out of Martham and set them on their way back to their parishes of origin. If people wished to move to another village or town to find work they had to have a certificate from their home parish saying they would be accepted back if they became unable to support themselves.

Many of the constables' duties involved petty crime. By the middle of the 19th century Norfolk's bad crime rate was largely caused by drunkenness. This may have been the result of the Beer Act of 1830 which made it possible for anyone to open a beer shop on payment of £2 and with three people as sureties.

Village constables were replaced by county police officers in 1856. Even so, Martham church's annual vestry meetings until 1894 were still nominating up to three people each year to act as constables. What their role was by that time was uncertain, but they sound like the forerunners of today's specials.

MATTISHALL

The revival in 1997 of a festive tradition stretching back 400 years attracted big crowds to this growing village a few miles from East Dereham. The Mattishall Gant was back on the calendar after a 20-year break and locals lined the streets to cheer on a noisy procession of floats and walkers.

The tradition began in 1588 after Norwich priest and Archbishop of Canterbury Matthew Parker married Margaret Harlestone from Mattishall. She was so relieved to wed after a seven-year wait that she gave instructions a sermon should be preached in her parish every year at Rogationtide by a Fellow of Parker's Cambridge College, Corpus Christi. The arrival of the eminent preacher, together with the beating of the bounds in Rogation week, sparked such celebrations that a fair sprang up, and so it continues today.

Great Ryburgh, near Fakenham, held a Gant in the village street until the early years of this century. It then moved to various meadows and continued until 1925.

MAUTBY

—— Although Yarmouth's holiday world is only a matter of miles away, the little village of Mautby retains a timeless quality among scattered smallholdings. The Domesday Book shows there was already a village here at the time of William the Conqueror with a mill and seven saltworks, an indication that the sea then reached much further inland.

By 1199 the lordship had passed from the Earl of Norfolk to the de Mauteby family, who held it until the reign of James I. Margaret, who married John Paston in 1440, was the daughter and heir of John de Mauteby and was raised at Mautby Hall. Many of the famous *Paston Letters* were written by and to her at Mautby, especially when she retired here after her husband's death. This collection of family correspondence is the earliest example of English letter-writing and gives a fascinating picture of domestic and public life during the Wars of the Roses. Two of Margaret's sons were engaged in the defence of nearby Caister Castle which had been bequeathed to the Pastons by Sir John Fastolf and was being besieged by the Duke of Norfolk. Margaret Paston was buried at Mautby church in the south aisle, which no longer exists. The thatched church with a round tower is set on a little hill among the fields, looking down on Mautby's proud history.

MELTON CONSTABLE

—— What amounted to a new town was built here in the 1880s at the junction of four railway lines linking Norfolk to the Midlands. In 30 years the population of this 'Crewe of Norfolk' increased tenfold and by 1911 it stood at nearly 1,200. Thereafter it slowly declined and Melton Constable's career as a rail centre was officially terminated. Between 1959 and 1964 British Railways closed the lines and withdrew both passenger and goods services. In 1971 the station was demolished while the works were converted into an industrial estate. Some say Melton Constable lies like a stranded whale in a vast agricultural area which has turned to other forms of transport. It certainly wears an air of lost glories.

In 1850 the consolidated parishes of Melton Constable and Burgh Parva had a population of just over 100. The railway companies which in 1893 became the Midland and Great Northern selected Melton as a major junction and depot. Four lines converged on it from Cromer, North Walsham, King's Lynn and Norwich. A station was built with a platform 800 feet long and a specially appointed waiting room for Lord Hastings, the local squire. This was followed by works for the construction of carriages, wagons and locomotives.

To the north-east of the station a new industrial village was created on a grid pattern of streets. About 170 new houses went up for railway workers, mainly in solid terraces and looking as if they had been transplanted from the industrial midlands. Residents were provided with corner shop facilities, a hotel, a school, a co-operative store and an institute for meetings and entertainments.

METHWOLD

The back-to-the-land movement in Victorian England took firm root for a time in a fertile corner of south-west Norfolk. A brookside site near Methwold was chosen for a fruit farm colony founded in 1889 by London businessman Robert Goodrich.

He believed it should be possible to live comfortably on the produce of two or three acres of land, provided the surplus could be sold directly to the customer. He left business in the capital to put his theories to the test with the Methwold Fruit Farm Colony. 'I had a good connection of friends in the City and obtained orders from them to take all the produce I could spare. I wrote to newspapers describing what I had done, and it was not long before shoals of letters came from people anxious to give up life in the town and settle on smallholdings in the country,' reported Goodrich.

Each colonist needed about £500 to get started, to cover purchase of land, building of houses, purchase of tools, seeds and fruit trees, and survival for up to two years before the holding began to bring in money. Fruit was the main product of the small farms and six years after the project was launched there was a small jam factory at Methwold. But steady income came from boxes of vegetables, fruit in season and new-laid eggs to customers in London at a fixed charge. There were even efforts to grow tobacco, and Goodrich's bee-keeping brother Frederick marketed the Norfolk Food of Strength, made from cereals and obviously a forerunner of today's health foods.

In May 1896 the colony's own newspaper, *The Methwold Express and Village Industries Gazette*, was launched with a special edition circulating in London. This was seen as an essential step forward to spread the gospel and to improve marketing methods. But in the decade before the First World War the dream faded, with marketing difficulties at the heart of ultimate failure.

Robert Goodrich claimed to live exclusively off his holding. Other colonists relied on private income, were retired or set up small industries unrelated to agriculture. In 1912 a post office was introduced and for simplicity's sake the colony name was changed to Brookville. Robert Goodrich died in 1917 and with him went the last vestige of those idealistic days. Since then, Brookville has evolved into a residential settlement scarcely related to the soil. But the name still echoes the pastoral impulse of over a century ago.

MILEHAM

An important piece of Norfolk history came to light here after being lost in undergrowth for decades. Experts were thrilled with the discovery of the remains of a Norman castle, just one of a handful of examples in the county of motte and bailey castles with masonry still standing.

The Normans enjoyed putting up symbols of their status after the triumphs of 1066, and Mileham Castle would have acted as a formidable power statement. Soldiers would have got stunning views across mid-Norfolk from the top of the stone keep. Probably two storeys high plus a basement, the keep was on top of the flat-topped nine-metre high motte (or mound). The remaining masonry of the keep, which has so excited experts, gives a fascinating insight into the scale of the structure. Limited excavation revealed floor tiles, brick fragments and small shards of mediaeval pottery. The stone walls are up to three metres thick, and as well as the keep there is also evidence of the inner and outer bailey, where there would have been a range of timber buildings, and the extra protection of moats and banks.

The Norfolk Monuments Management Project unearthed the remains which were covered by a wilderness of trees, scrub and nettles. Even many local people in this area north-west of East Dereham were unaware of the existence of such an important Norman castle. It is extremely rare for any stone to have been left from Norman castles as most were plundered after the structures were emptied. Mileham Castle was built around 1100 and was owned by the Fitzalan family until 1559. King Stephen probably seized it for a short time in the mid-12th century before returning it to the Fitzalans by the Treaty of Westminster in 1153. The Manor of Mileham belonged to the Coke family of Holkham for many years. There is public access to the castle site.

MUNDESLEY

Past and present mingle easily in a confined space on Mundesley seafront a few miles from Cromer. Probably the smallest museum in Britain opened in 1995 in the old coastguard lookout point. There's just over 100 square feet of display space on the ground floor and 60 square feet on the floor above. Visitors are rationed to no more than five up and five down at any given point.

The ground floor holds photographs, prints and information illustrating Mundesley's maritime history from the beginning of the last century, lifeboat activity from 1811 to 1895 and the present inshore boat as well as the growth of the village as a seaside attraction. Exhibits include the station records, rocket pistols, breeches buoy and foghorn.

The first floor has been reinstated as a coastguard lookout of the 1930–40 era, containing items such as a tide clock and sighting scope. It also displays modern equipment – radar, VHF radio, as the National Coastwatch Institution, with the approval of Mundesley Parish Council, has renewed visual watches, providing a service for bathers, windsurfers and occupants of small boats, being in direct touch with the inshore lifeboat. The museum is open at Easter and at weekends from May to September.

NARBOROUGH

An old red-roofed farm shed is the last link between this growing village five miles west of Swaffham and a bustling First World War aerodrome. The shed stands defiantly in a field next to the Contract Wood, set back from the Marham road, and is the only remaining building of over 100 that once formed one of the biggest aerodromes in the county. It was used by the airmen as a YMCA centre.

Another relic from the same period, the fondly-remembered Black Hangar, was demolished in 1977 after fierce gales had ripped off part of the roof. For many years it had followed a familiar pattern across Norfolk and been used as an agricultural store, but in its heyday it provided shelter for many of Britain's early service aircraft.

About 30 airfields were established in Norfolk at the start of the First World War, most of them small landing grounds of less than 100 acres. Spreading over a staggering 908 acres, more than a quarter of the parish, Narborough was one of the biggest in the county. Compared to the massive present-day base at nearby RAF Marham, Narborough may seem insignificant, but by First World War standards it was a large concern while Marham itself was then only a small site of some 80 acres.

In 1914 the Royal Naval Air Service, formed by the Admiralty, was mainly responsible for the defence of this country against Zeppelin attacks. It soon became clear that if the RNAS station at

South Denes in Great Yarmouth was to offer any kind of resistance to German air-raids it must have in the vicinity a number of emergency landing grounds available for use day and night. Narborough's role as a satellite of the South Denes station began in August 1915, and the first 'plane to land there is thought to have been an Avro 504. It was certainly a two-seater as a joy-ride was given to at least one lucky local! Narborough was transferred to the Royal Flying Corps the following year and hundreds of airmen formed the biggest invasion the village had ever seen.

Captain W.E. Johns, author of the Biggles adventure stories about a World War I fighter pilot, picked up some of his flying knowledge at Narborough. He lived for a time at Sporle before the war and worked as a sanitary inspector for Swaffham Rural District Council. As a yeomanry trooper in 1914 he was mobilised and later transferred to the Royal Flying Corps at Narborough before going to France. Narborough is mentioned in his book *Biggles and the Camel Squadron*.

NEW BUCKENHAM

It all began when William D'Albini gave his castle in Old Buckenham to the Augustinians in about 1145. While they used the materials to construct their priory, he selected a more prosperous location beside the Norwich to Thetford road. Here William built a new fortification, and immediately east of this the village was laid out as a planned settlement on a grid of intersecting streets with its own market to raise dues for the castle.

It is unique in England as a mediaeval planned town which has maintained its original size and plan intact. It was bounded by the Town Ditch, parts of which were widened in the 19th century to serve the tanning industry, and are still clearly visible behind The Grange and The Rookery. The tightly-knit streets are lined with 16th-century timber-framed houses.

New Buckenham Castle consists of an inner bailey and two outer baileys, and the keep is the earliest and probably the largest circular one in the country. Just inside the south-west bailey stood the Castle Chapel of St Mary, converted into a barn after the Dissolution. The inner bailey is circular and surrounded by a water-filled moat from which steeply-wooded ramparts rise to over 40 feet. Steps up the ramparts enable visitors to walk round the top of the earthworks.

Carved out from adjoining parishes to provide valuable grazing land for the new settlement in the late 12th century, New Buckenham Common still survives intact, one of the largest in Norfolk. It is lightly grazed by cattle kept by the owners of grazing rights and a pinder is appointed to look after the livestock during the summer months.

NORTH WALSHAM

The bells pealed out for many hours from the great tower of the parish church standing guard over the market square. North Walsham revelled in its Ascension Day Fayre on Friday, 15th May 1724.

The following morning at 9 o'clock the tower of St Nicholas' suddenly collapsed without warning. The vicar, the Rev Thomas Jeffrey, entered the catastrophe in the parish register: 'Memorandum May 16. Between 9 and 10 o'clock in the forenoon on the Sat. fell down the north and south sides of the steeple, and no person we hear of yet getting any mischief thereby. Thanks be to God for his goodness therein.'

The gaunt ruin asking for attention as you approach the north Norfolk town is all that is left of a tower and spire which once rose to twice its existing height. The tower was once 147 feet tall, with a spire which took its total height to about 170 feet – the tallest construction in the county except for Norwich Cathedral spire. It contained a heavy peal of five, perhaps six, bells, and a chiming clock. The rooftop was surrounded by a square battlemented parapet with a statue of one of the four evangelists at each corner. The roof was drained at each corner by one of four gargoyles, two of which remain standing at the foot of the tower.

A tower rebuilding fund was launched in 1749, but other than one entry in a churchwarden's book there is no record of any attempt at restoration. For a century the tower stood like this

North Walsham's ruined church tower.

until 1835 when a few small falls proved the weakness of the upper stonework. The following year saw the last major fall when on Wednesday, 17th February 1836 at 6 o'clock heavy wintry gales brought down the north side of the steeple. The immediate area of the town experienced the sensation of an earthquake. This left the east wall of the tower threatening to collapse onto the church. Fifty feet were soon removed as a safety precaution, and that gave the tower the familiar shape seen today – a ragged warden of the fine church under its wing.

NORWICH

Down an alley between the high rise flats of bustling Rouen Road and the red-light district of King Street stands the church of St Julian, a faithful reconstruction of the mediaeval building destroyed by a German bomb in 1942.

Built into the north wall is a Norman doorway rescued from

Mother Julian's shrine down a Norwich alleyway.

the church of St Michael at Thorn in nearby Ber Street which had suffered the same fate. It leads to the shrine to Mother Julian, the 14th-century authoress of *Revelations of Divine Love*, the first known English book written by a woman. It was in 1373 that she lay dying in a room somewhere in Norwich. Then, after receiving the Last Rites, she gazed upon the cross and God's love became known to her in a series of revelations or 'showings' as she preferred to call them. Moved by these experiences and a return to health, the woman withdrew from the world, taking refuge in an anchorite cell attached to St Julian's church overlooking the river Wensum. She remained in prayer and contemplation until her death in 1413.

She wrote down the first abbreviated account of her showings at the time, but many years of reflection passed before she understood their meaning sufficiently to produce the longer version known as *The Sixteen Revelations of Divine Love*. It was not uncommon in the Middle Ages for men and women to shut themselves away. Anchorites and anchoresses had to satisfy the bishop as to their purity of character. They were then taken to a secluded building from which they emerged only on death. In Norwich there were anchorages at most of the gates and bridges and in some of the churches.

Julian's view of God as 'Our Mother' led to her being adopted as patron of the movement for the ordination of women into the priesthood.

OLD BUCKENHAM

Hollywood came to south Norfolk when an extension to the village hall at Old Buckenham, south of Attleborough, was opened by film star James Stewart in 1983.

The 453rd Bomb Group Memorial Room was paid for by group members, and inside is a plaque, roll of honour and their memorabilia. It was an emotional return for the Hollywood legend.

From March 1944 James Stewart was the group's Operations Officer, and while he was there one of the group's squadrons, the 733rd, set an unbeaten record of 82 missions without loss. What remains of the old airfield, most of the main runway, some of the perimeter track and the odd hut, lies to the north-east of the village. Though much of the airfield has been returned to farming part of the original runway is still used by light aircraft. By the end of the last war there were 37 operational airfields in Norfolk.

Few would disagree that James Stewart was the most famous personality to be stationed over here – although another Hollywood star also served at Old Buckenham under his real name of Walter Matasschauskayasky. He became better known as Walter Matthau.

OULTON

This pretty little village three miles from Aylsham – not to be confused with ever-growing Oulton Broad just over the border in Suffolk – remembers airmen who served there in the last war with a memorial at the crossroads north of the parish. It is built of red brick with a plaque of Cumbrian stone inscribed: 'RAF Oulton 1940–1945. In grateful tribute to those members of the British Commonwealth and American Air Forces who served at RAF Oulton and in honour of those that gave their lives. Those who died for our freedom will live forever in our hearts'. The memorial was dedicated in 1994.

An area of farmland was cleared at the start of the summer of 1940 to make a dispersal base for aircraft based at nearby Horsham St Faith, where they had Blenheim bombers. When the first airmen arrived they were billeted in cattle sheds at Green Farm. Soon after this a number of Nissen huts were erected. To most local residents the base was known as 'Bluestone Drome' after the name of the railway halt and level crossing adjoining the airfield. All public roads around and inside the airfield boundary remained open to the public during those early days. After reconstruction work in 1943–44, a number of roads were closed and it became almost impossible to reach the village from the south side.

Nearby Blicking Hall, now a popular National Trust property, was taken over for officers' quarters. It is said the Oulton Station Commander had the use of a bedroom once kept for the visits of Anne Boleyn! As well as enjoying the glories of the building, woods, park and lake, the men for a time had the company of film stars Margaret Lockwood and Patricia Roc. Blicking Hall was the backdrop for scenes in 'The Wicked Lady'.

For a couple of years after the war Oulton hangars were used for storage and maintenance of Mosquito aircraft, some of which were supplied to other air forces overseas. Then, in scenes repeated across several Norfolk airfields, turkey-rearing sheds took over the concrete runways and most of the land returned to agricultural use.

OXNEAD

The Pastons, mediaeval gentry of exceptional drive and talent, emerged from the coastal village that bears their name to become the dominant family in the county for over two centuries. Their most luxurious house was Oxnead Hall, built above the river Bure three miles south-east of Aylsham. It became run down in the 18th century and when Lord Anson bought the bulk of the estate as an investment it was demolished except for its kitchen wing, that the size of a substantial manor house. It is remembered mainly for its role in entertaining King Charles II on his visit to Norfolk in 1671.

After leaving Norwich and paying a visit to Blickling Hall, Charles drove the few miles to Oxnead, the home of his devoted supporter Sir Robert Paston, leader of the Royalist party in Norfolk. He had built a splendid new banqueting hall in anticipation of the royal visit. Charles made no secret of his pleasure in exchanging the rather hollow hospitality of Blickling for the sincere loyalty and devotion which awaited him at Oxnead. It was there that he told his host that Norfolk ought to be 'cut out in slips, to make roads for the rest of the kingdom.' This has sometimes been taken as a compliment on the excellence of the Norfolk highways, but it may have been intended as a satire on the flatness of the Norfolk countryside or even as a comment of the aridity on much of its soil.

In his grand new banqueting hall Sir Robert Paston entertained the King and court to 'a most sumptuous supper which cost him three times more than Earles' daughters had heretofore unto their portions; provisions superabundantly plentiful and all accommodations answerable.' So Paston's chaplain described the banquet in the sermon preached 12 years later at his funeral. Next day the Queen completed the joy of the loyal Pastons by driving out from Norwich and joining the King at dinner. After the meal the King set out to visit Lord Townshend, the Lord Lieutenant of the county, at Raynham, while the Queen stayed a little longer at Oxnead, playing at cards with her hostess and court ladies.

PLUMSTEAD

While Great and Little Plumstead have been turned into sizeable dormitories a few miles east of Norwich, plain Plumstead snoozes gently and retains considerable charm deep in the north Norfolk countryside. It snuggles between Little Barningham and Baconsthorpe on the road leading to Holt, new homes blending sympathetically among the old.

Although Plumstead means 'dwelling site near the plums', the village used to have a pub called the Cherry Tree. It is now a private house with homes also taking over the old bowling green. A colourful and unusual salute to the past can be found at the tastefully restored Old Post Office – there's a painting of a Penny Black stamp attached to the wall.

St Michael's parish church dates from the 12th century and is one of several in the area with a Nelson connection. The Rev Benjamin Suckling, Rector of Plumstead and Matlaske from 1793 until 1837, is buried in the chancel. He was a cousin of Nelson, whose mother, Catherine Suckling, was the daughter of the Rev Maurice Suckling, Prebendary of Westminster and Rector of Barsham and Woodton, near Beccles. There's no rectory here and Mr Suckling probably lived at Aylsham.

All the church walls are built of flintstones gathered from the fields. Construction of the north wall shows its age in a fascinating way. The flints and ironstone are laid in horizontal courses and herringboned in the lower and more western part of the wall. This is Norman work from the early 12th century. The upper part of the wall and the chancel do not show this regularity in building. So we know the original church was a small, low building while additions were made eastwards and upwards. Near the south door there is a scratch dial, a primitive form of sundial.

POTTER HEIGHAM

Boats and holidaymakers may dominate this part of the Broadland beat during the summer months, but Potter Heigham has also become famous as the home of the most beloved of

Norfolk humorists. Sidney Grapes was born in the village in 1888 and lived there all his life.

The son of a local builder and carpenter, he opened a bicycle shop which grew into a garage. It was here, in his little office beside the narrow hump-backed bridge spanning the river Thurne, that he pinned up one December a notice that read: 'A merry Christmas to all my customers what hev paid their bills, and a prosperous New Year to them what hent.' He developed in middle life a great gift as a Norfolk dialect comedian, and he became a favourite on concert platforms, the stage and radio all over East Anglia.

Then, at Christmas 1946, in the bleak aftermath of the war, he was inspired to write to the main local paper, the *Eastern Daily Press*, the first of a series of letters signed 'The Boy John'. People clamoured for more and Sidney, working intermittently as the spirit moved him, kept up the supply until his death in 1958. He assumed the character of a rustic who wrote as he spoke and spelled as he pleased. The Boy John Letters, drawn from the heart of village life, were circulated and enjoyed all over the world wherever East Anglians had settled. They remain fresh and popular, gracing countless Norfolk functions calling for a spot of honest local humour.

Potter Heigham became known as The Boy John's village and some still call it such today. Sidney Grapes was as endearing a character as any created in his writing. A keen servant of the village and its church, he was a chorister in his boyhood and a faithful churchwarden until the end of his days. By his wish, the church was decorated at his funeral as if for a spring festival and happy hymns were sung. An oak vestry was built in his memory.

PUDDING NORTON

Just a mile or so outside Fakenham in the meadow beside Pudding Norton Hall are the earthworks of a fine example of a deserted village, together with the ruins of the parish church. The village of Nortuna, as it was originally called, decayed gradually with the population decline of the 15th and 16th centuries.

The farm track running north to south through the meadow is the line of the village street, while the banks and ditches running away at right angles from it are the toft or property divisions within the village. Little trace of the houses remains above ground because they were made of either timber or clay. The only mediaeval building to survive is the church of St Margaret which was 'dilapidated' before 1602. And all that remains here is part of the tower with the top like a broken tooth and a base worn into hollows by cattle.

A closer examination of the pattern of the village earthworks suggests there was an element of planning in the layout. Several boundary banks on one side of the street are directly opposite similar ones on the other side. There is also a certain uniformity of width, and several of the larger tofts have rear banks an equal distance from the street.

QUARLES

A handful of homes, stately chestnut trees, one farm – and a community spirit second to none! That sums up picturesque little Quarles as it ignores the pressures and pace of the modern world. Gloriously alone on the edge of the Holkham Estate a few miles from Wells, it is hard to find and difficult to leave if you like small settlements cloaked in tranquillity.

Senior resident, retired farm worker Norman Dack, moved to Quarles from Creake a couple of miles up the road in 1945. 'We have no shop, pub, church or chapel. There's no street lighting. But this is an old-fashioned community. We all know each other and we all help each other.' Not too difficult a task, perhaps, with a population of only 20, but still refreshing and reassuring to hear in fast-changing times. When Norman started work on Quarles Farm, the horse was still king and he had a score of men and boys beside him on the land. Three of his neighbours are now employed on the farm. A few more signposts put up recently have cut down the number of lorry drivers getting lost in the vicinity. Busiest time of the year for visitors to Quarles is when the chestnuts fall from the trees that keep guard over one of Norfolk's tiniest hamlets.

Another dot on the map demands attention just down the lane. Waterden does have a church and a former rectory now offering bed and breakfast, but all the parish land has been worked as one farm since the enclosures. The population has always been small, reaching a peak of 44 in the middle of the 19th century. The church of All Saints is in the middle of rolling fields with a neat path cut to its Norman doorways. Occasional services are still held in this building, restored after being badly damaged by the great gale of 1895. Standing in the porch and looking north you can imagine a route down the hill to the site of the mediaeval village just to the left of the farm buildings.

RACKHEATH

A good two miles out of this fast-expanding suburb of Norwich stands All Saints' church in glorious isolation. Down a twisting lane and overlooking rolling agricultural acres, it proclaims a stirring revival story.

The church was declared redundant in 1971 and rapidly fell into ruin. A leaking roof, smashed windows and font and countless other signs of decay could easily have led to demolition, but a small band of people resolved that All Saints should be saved. Several alternative uses were mooted before it came under the wing of the Norfolk Churches Trust in 1976. Since then a programme of services and fund-raising events has been held to transform the picture. Small repairs have been carried out alongside major improvements. The whole interior has been redecorated. It still has no heating or electricity and services are held regularly by candlelight.

It is thought the village was once situated around this church. Why the population moved away and left it alone in the fields remains a cause for debate. The conclusion that the Black Death wiped out the community is a little too obvious. There could have been many other reasons – the drying up of the source of water, for example. Even so, American airmen from Rackheath airfield during the last war claimed that signs of former houses could be seen from above at certain seasons showing as crop marks in the surrounding fields.

When the church was built early in the 14th century there were two villages – Rackheath Magna and Rackheath Parva which had its own rector and church of Holy Trinity. Of this church no signs remain, although it is said to have existed somewhere in Rackheath Park on a piece of land known as Chapel Yard. The Pettus family were at Rackheath from 1591 until 1722, owning Rackheath Hall (not the present building). Important merchants, they provided mayors and sheriffs of Norwich. One was an MP and three became High Sheriffs of Norfolk. Many of the memorials in All Saints at Rackheath are those of the Pettus family. The Straceys built the present hall and also made great improvements to the church after taking over the estate in 1780.

ROUDHAM

This small Breckland village houses one of the most evocative ruins in the county – the result of an accident over 250 years ago.

On 10th August 1736 plumbers were at work repairing the lead on the top of the tower of St Andrew's church when one of them blew the ashes out of his pipe. These fell on the thatch and fire destroyed the greater part of the church. Tradition records that an appeal for subscriptions for its repair received such a generous response that the treasurer did a runner with the proceeds.

The strange and haunting beauties of Roudham's landmark ruin have never been better captured than in Olive Cook's 1956 book on Breckland: 'Then suddenly, above a group of tiny red-brick cottages framed by lime and elm, a decaying flint tower adorned with a monstrous fish-eyed gargoyle appears against the sky. Enough of the tower survives to show that it must once have been extremely graceful. There are remains of a pretty parapet, and the entrance to the church, which was under the tower, is surmounted by a charming cusped niche and a circular opening. A great bush half covers the doorway and the threshold is deep in nettles which seem to have thrived undisturbed for many years. They have taken complete possession of the west end of the nave.

'Grasses, poppies and dog daisies ripple up to the chancel where the superb arch of the east window, which alone stands entire, spans the space between the decomposing, ivy-matted walls. Elder bushes flank the nave, and at the season when they flower their white disks shine out against the dark undergrowth and the ruin walls as bright lamps must once have glowed in the dusk of the church. To the west, beyond the tower, a rude triangle of flint, pierced by a narrow, creeper-curtained opening, and an iron railing mark the enclosure where rest members of the Boyce family. Their tombs and monuments are almost concealed by the vigorous growth of the nettles.'

ROUGHTON

A genius found sanctuary in a wooden hut a few miles from Cromer after taking flight from Nazi threats in Germany. Professor Albert Einstein, famous for his Theory of Relativity, arrived in Norfolk in early September 1933. He told a local newspaper reporter: 'All I want is peace, and could I have found a more peaceful retreat than here in England?'

His host was Commander Oliver Stillingfleet Locker-Lampson, barrister and journalist and MP for the Handsworth division of Birmingham. He owned property in Norfolk, including a hotel in Cromer and land at Roughton Heath on which there were several wooden buildings. This camp at the end of a lane was surrounded by trees, and the site was off the Thorpe Market to Northrepps road.

Although many people knew Einstein was in Norfolk, and he received plenty of visitors, including newsmen, efforts were made to keep strangers away. Albert Thurston and his father-in-law, Herbert Eastoe, a gamekeeper on the nearby Gunton Estate, acted as armed guards. Women secretaries to the great man were also armed. The camp had no deliveries. When food was needed the Commander and secretaries would take the car and go shopping, presumably in Cromer and Sheringham. Milk was obtained from a couple of goats. Occasionally Einstein would walk over the Heath to do some shopping at Roughton Post Office.

Although most sources suggest he stayed at Roughton for about a month – September 1933 – there are pointers to a much longer sojourn. He was given a surprise birthday party, with a cake made by Mrs Eastoe. Einstein's birthday was in March. Albert Thurston said: 'I would say he was here for the best part of twelve months. He was a very nice, quiet man who was always talking about the country. He always had his walking stick, but he never wore socks. He told me his big toe made holes in the socks, so he never wore them.'

One of Einstein's illustrious callers in Norfolk was sculptor Jacob Epstein, who began a bust of the great mathematician and physicist in three sittings in one of the huts.

SALTHOUSE

One of the victims of the devastating floods of 1953 was a spectacular castle-like structure on Salthouse beach in north Norfolk. It was the work of local-boy-made-good Onesiphorous Randall, born at Cley just along the coast in 1798.

He went to London, became a speculative builder and in keeping with his Christian name – it means 'bringing profit' – amassed a fortune. On his triumphant return to Norfolk he bought woodlands in Holt, now part of Gresham's School, where he lived for a time before moving to Kelling Old Hall on becoming Lord of the Manor.

The building on Salthouse beach made sure he would not be forgotten. Although generally known as Randall's Folly, the locals had a much more descriptive name because of the entertaining of ladies that went on there. After Randall's death in 1873, it was bought by the Board of Trade for use by the Coastguard Service. With rocket and lifesaving apparatus kept there it also became known as the Rocket House, complete with breeches buoy training pole on the beach where regular practices were held much to the interest of residents and visitors alike. After the First World War it was sold as a private house, had a new wing built on in 1937 and continued in use, with a break for military lookout purposes during the last war, as a holiday home until 1953 when the floods took away much of the beach and house as well.

SCARNING

Extensive development has just about turned this into an overspill village on East Dereham's doorstep! Certainly, it all seems rather at odds with the description of 'Arcady' given to Scarning by Dr Augustus Jessopp who cared for his rural parish for over 30 years. He died in 1914.

This outstanding historian, essayist and country parson was headmaster at King Edward VI School in Norwich before he became Rector of Scarning and deeply concerned about Norfolk labourers languishing in poverty. He wrote *Arcady For Better For Worse* after gaining the ear and then the confidence of surly and suspicious villagers, and they inspired some of his most powerful writing. For example, he struck up an unlikely liaison with 'Loafing Ben', a burly ne'er-do-well who scraped a sort of living as a casual labourer. Jessopp called at the homestead: 'His old parents were fading out of life, the vital spark in the mere ashes that remained gleaming every now and then, and twinkling, when a human dust was stirred by a basin of broth or a drop of some stimulant. They were feebly cowering over the shadow of a fire in the miserable shanty, and as I sat with them and felt my way by speaking of "such things as pass human understanding", I fancied I saw the semblance of faint emotion in one or the other. Somehow I found myself kneeling down upon the mud floor.'

An Arcadian Club to promote more interest in Jessopp's work has been formed, one of its aims being to restore the graves of Augustus and his wife Margaret in Scarning churchyard. Most meetings of these enthusiasts are in the village hall. Jessopp organised the opening of this building in 1902 when among the worthies on parade was fellow-writer Henry Rider Haggard, born a few miles away at West Bradenham.

SEDGEFORD

When they point to 'The Magazine' in this village on the road between Docking and Heacham they are turning some fascinating pages of history centred on the Civil War. The

Magazine House, now a Grade II listed private dwelling, was used by the Royalist Sir Hamon L'Estrange as a store for ammunition. The Hunstanton family tried, gallantly and obstinately but with only limited success, to offer some resistance on the King's behalf against the overwhelming power of the Parliamentary supporters of Norfolk.

At the outbreak of the Civil War, Sir Hamon was nearly 60, full of vigour and loyally supported in all his enterprises by his wife Alice, daughter of Richard Stubbe of Sedgeford. The whole family displayed their Royalist sympathies openly and provocatively from the very beginning of the troubles, culminating in the siege of King's Lynn in 1643 after the town declared for the King and Sir Hamon was appointed Governor. The Magazine House, set back on the left hand side as you leave Sedgeford towards Docking, looks more ecclesiastic than military. It is an elegant two-storey building with stone quoins, parapets and mullioned windows tucked discreetly between two chimneys.

Sedgeford Hall is an attractive Queen Anne house built of yellow brick. On some cottages in the village there are terracotta plaques made by the gifted lady of the manor at the end of the last century.

SEETHING

Plenty of traditional charm here with several thatched buildings, including the parish church, and a mere where children feed the ducks and older residents remember when the Americans came.

An airfield was built in 1941 and this village nine miles south of Norwich became home to the 448th Bomb Group who flew B24 Liberators. There were 3,000 men on base and links were forged with locals that remain strong over half a century later. Generous gifts for the village church and school have marked recent years and there have been emotional returns from former airmen. Memorials were dedicated in 1984 to all the men killed flying from here. They are placed in Seething churchyard and on the airfield now owned by Waveney Flying Group. The old control tower has been restored and is open once a month during the summer. Beside it stands a memorial to all based at Station 146 between 1943 and 1945.

Seething School records for 23rd November 1943 report: 'The whole school received an invitation from the American airbase to celebrate Thanksgiving Day by provision of a party given by the officers and men.' There was great excitement as trucks arrived to pick up the pupils and teachers; at that time 85 local children and two evacuees attended the school.

Pat Everson, a schoolgirl of nine when the Americans arrived, started the 448th Bomb Group Collection in 1984 by writing to all men stationed at Seething for their personal stories, photographs and documents. Two years of fund-raising in the USA and hard work in Norfolk paid off with the reopening of the control tower. Since then the Station 146 Tower Association has been formed, with newsletters going round the world and special tower open days attracting big crowds.

SHIMPLING

Unemployment and poverty were constant enemies in Norfolk's agricultural communities as traditional farming methods were altered by the rise of mechanisation. The 1820s brought dramatic confrontations, not least in the little village of Shimpling, near Diss.

Discontent spilled over into violence in 1822 when it became clear a local farmer intended to use a threshing machine, powered by a horse, to speed up the process with less labour. Seeing their livelihoods at risk, 'large bodies of labourers assembled in the parishes of Shimpling, Gissing and Burston, and broke in pieces the threshing machines in three parishes.' They moved on to Diss 'and manifested great disposition to riot and mischief.' The ringleaders of the Diss riot came from Shimpling and were bailed to appear at the next sitting of the Quarter Sessions at Norwich. Such was agitation in the city that the hearing had to be postponed and extra militia men were drafted in to keep the peace. James Sparham, a Burston farmer, had given orders to his servant to take a machine to Shimpling. He was met by 50 men who openly declared they were out to prevent any threshing machine from entering the village.

Sparham, confident the law was on his side, ordered the machine forward, but before it crossed the parish boundary the rioters seized the horses and removed them from the shafts. Armed with hatchets, pickaxes, hooks and large cudgels, the Shimpling men made short work of the threshing machine. Mr Sparham took out his notebook and wrote down the names of the rioters before riding on.

Robert Chatten was named as ringleader, and although the judge recommended him for merciful consideration on account of his youth, he was sent to prison for 12 months, fined £5 and bound over in the sum of £100 himself with two additional sureties of £50 to keep the peace for two years. James Goddard also came in for a harsh sentence, mainly because he had to be restrained from 'committing an act of outrage on the person of the magistrate acting in suppression of the riot.' Mr Sparham spoke up for the other four who were treated more leniently.

It was obvious that proceedings against the Shimpling Six were treated as a show trial. While that may have been the end of the Shimpling affair, it was by no means the end of disturbances in south Norfolk.

SHOTESHAM

—— A leading surgeon of his day, William Fellowes founded the Norfolk and Norwich Hospital in 1771, a few years after setting up what is thought to be the first cottage hospital in the country at Shotesham, an attractive if scattered village six miles south of the city.

He bought Shotesham Park and the estates in 1731 and built a house of industry, often referred to as a workhouse, to accommodate the poor of the parish and to give them something to do. He also set up in Shotesham a cold water bath, his 'water cure' for parishioners, before his infirmary brought more local fame. It had room for a dozen patients while across the road was accommodation for doctors and nurses and a house for the mentally disturbed. The cottage hospital still stands as a private house called Oakwood, and the old workhouse is now called Henstead Cottage.

Henry Howard, Earl of Northampton, was born in the village completely by chance in February 1539. Frances, wife of Henry, Earl of Surrey, was passing through Shotesham on her way from Bungay Castle when she realised her time had come. She stopped her carriage outside Grove Farm House and Henry was born soon after. He gave his name to the charity which still brings help and happiness to the village.

A few hundred yards from All Saints' church at Shotesham, on the Brooke road, stand a row of eight cottages and a central hall. They were built in 1879 for eight local bachelors or widowers of good character. For many years only men were allowed to live in the cottages, completely modernised in 1960, but rules have been relaxed in more recent times to allow married couples and single women to live there.

Also in 1879, trustees of the Earl of Northampton's charity, the Mercers' Company of London, decided to build a hospital in Shotesham so that no-one need leave the parish. Opened in 1885, the Trinity Hospital has the Earl's coat of arms and that of the Mercers' Company on the front wall and entrance gate.

 ## SHROPHAM

A squire's wife determined to show rural plight rather than rustic charm used the isolated village of Shropham, five miles south-west of Attleborough, as the setting for her most celebrated stories at the turn of the century.

Mary Mann, a prolific novelist, shocked her readers in *The Fields of Dulditch* with brutal accounts of the life of labouring families at a time when such poverty was not only commonplace but seemingly incurable. These harrowing chapters are a considerable challenge to any cosy, nostalgic visions we may still harbour about the 'good old days'.

Born in Norwich, she settled in Shropham on marrying in 1871. Her husband Fairman Mann farmed 800 acres in and around the village and assumed the role of caring squire. His wife helped teach reading at the village school, organised school treats and was a frequent visitor to the labourers' spartan homes. When her husband died in 1913 Mary Mann took a house at

Winterton and finally moved to Sheringham. She died in 1929.

D.H. Lawrence was an admirer of her work. The brutality of labourers to their wives and children is starkly prominent in her depiction of Norfolk village life, and she also dealt with serious problems confronting farmers. Her first novel, *The Parish of Hilby*, includes an episode about a young farmer coping with a strike on his farm, while *Moonlight* opens with the suicide of a bankrupt farmer.

 ## SISLAND

This tiny parish of under 500 acres just west of Loddon has a big reputation for giving nature a hand.

Since the early 1980s plants and wildlife in St Mary's churchyard have been carefully protected and catalogued by parishioners, and the churchyard is officially declared a conservation area by the Norfolk Naturalists' Trust. In 1989 Sisland (pronounced 'Sizzland' or 'Sizeland') was selected for the national launch of 'The Living Churchyard' project. Prince Charles sent a special message to be read on that proud occasion, and since then the village has become the focus of attention from all over the country and abroad.

Slow worms have been found, while a swallowtail butterfly has been seen in gardens opposite. Spotted flycatchers nest in the ivy and marsh harriers and three species of owl are seen regularly in the village. Green woodpeckers are returning and a bat box has been placed in the churchyard.

Badly damaged by lightning in 1761, although the thatch was untouched, St Mary's was presented with a Norfolk Society award in 1989, and soon after named the county's Tourist's Church of the Year for a parish with a thousand inhabitants or less. Sunday services are held each month.

An archaeological investigation in the church was part of a major project to survey the parish and discover as much of its early history as possible. Earliest finds to date include Neolithic flint tools and Bronze Age metalwork. Sisland has an impressive selection of buildings, including the mediaeval hall of White House (originally Sisland Hall) and a probable moated manor house at the east end of the parish complete with the remains of a large fishpond constructed to provide fresh food.

🌿 SOUTH CREAKE

Now an attractive haven for the retired a few miles from Fakenham, this was once a veritable hive of industry and innovation. Biggest clue to such a lively past is a complex of buildings with a tall tower on the main street, a former brewery, dwellings and a large house that was the Chequers Inn.

The brewery was there in the reign of George II (1727–1760). *White's Directory of Norfolk* for 1836 shows John Oliver, brewer and maltster, and the Oliver family owned the site until the 1890s. The parish magazine for August 1898 reported that the month would always be memorable for the burning down of the brewery 'which, calamitous as it was, might have proved much more serious had not the wind fallen'. The fire and damage to the tower may well have signalled the end of the Oliver enterprise for by 1900 J. Pinchin was the owner. He went out of business in 1915 and part of the Warwickshire Regiment was billeted on the site during the First World War.

In 1921 the premises were bought by George Money, a cabinet maker from London. He installed electric lighting. Power was produced from a fairground generator driven by a gas engine converted to run on kerosene, as there was no mains gas supply. Here he founded the Ace Razor Blade Company. Soft Sheffield steel ribbon was delivered in coils. A long wooden shed was built on the other side of the road to accommodate an electrical hardening process, incorporating Mr Money's secret method of 'meths dripping'. The hardened strip was passed through a conduit under the road to machines in the tower. The strip was perforated, tempered, hollow ground, cleaned for an acid printing stage, cut into blades and rounded at the ends. The finished blades were wrapped and packed in the cottage at the side of the main entrance. George Money was out to produce British blades as good as imported ones. He used several brand names. 'All British' were supplied to the forces during the last war.

When the Alley brothers, Eric and John, left the village, taking their Farmers Glory wheatflakes to larger premises in Huntingdon, George Money stepped into the market and produced his own breakfast cereal, Myflakes. A plant for producing gas was installed over the road. Gas was pumped under it to fire a large rotary oven for toasting the flakes. As the business developed a mill was installed for grinding meal. Bread and cakes, baked in the ovens at the rear of the site, were delivered by horse and cart. George Money died in 1951, and the razor blade business finished. His son, Fred Money, sold the brewery and the site to property developers. The main building stood empty for years although most of the machinery was intact until the early 1970s. Some of it was passed to the Norfolk Rural Life Museum at Gressenhall to form one of their exhibitions of Norfolk industry.

The Alley brothers took over as tenants of Bluestone Farm in South Creake in 1930 – and it became famous as the first fully mechanised farm in England. The first two Massey Harris combines to enter the country were imported in time for the first harvest. The farm was running at a profit after two years, but new methods eliminated the need for what had been the biggest labour force in the village. The brothers started the wheatflakes factory to give back some of the jobs – but moved on when the venture proved such a big success.

SPORLE

Hidden in a valley off the ever-busy A47, it would be easy to dismiss Sporle as a rather colourless dormitory alongside historic and attractive neighbours, Swaffham and Castle Acre. But this village, combined with the practically deserted parishes of Great and Little Palgrave, does have intriguing stories to tell. For a start, there's the open dyke that runs almost the length of the village. Tradition has it that no-one can be regarded as 'true Sporle' unless they have fallen in at least once.

The 13th-century church dominates the scene. Although it is dedicated to St Mary, it is the wall paintings of St Catherine that have attracted attention from afar. Still virtually intact although faded, they tell in strip cartoon style the life story of the saint whose name lives on in the Catherine Wheel, the instrument of torture by which she died.

The playing field now occupies the site where once stood Sporle Priory, founded in the reign of Henry II. Benedictine monks lived here for 200 years, and it was a cell to the Abbey of St Florence at Saumers in the diocese of Anges in the province of Anjou in France. During the wars with France it was in the hands of the Crown. It was valued at 8/6d in 1291 with possessions in four parishes. It was dissolved in 1416.

STIFFKEY

The dreamer came face to face with reality in 1937 when Henry Williamson stopped writing romantic novels about Devon and became a Norfolk farmer. He invested his entire capital in the small and run-down Old Castle Farm at Stiffkey in north Norfolk.

He had scarcely an idea about working the land and his adventures are told, not without humour, in *The Story of a Norfolk Farm*, first published in 1941 and dedicated 'to all who have worked and suffered for the land and the people of Great Britain'.

Williamson had explored the county on a bicycle in 1912, but the later decision to move east came after a chance meeting with his publisher and friend Dick de la Mare, son of the poet, who already had a country home in Norfolk.

Eventually, Williamson became disenchanted with some local people who spread rumours about his being in league with Germany, and suggested that even the skylights in his studio were arranged in such a way so as to signal to Luftwaffe navigators. He returned to Devon and wrote 17 more books.

On his departure, he wrote: 'As I look back on the last two years, I am glad they will not come again. For one period of about three months, I thought I would not be able to keep on. During those months I worked on the farm by day, taught myself the building trade, drove the tractor, was continually striving to give others a new outlook, and often wrote until one or two o'clock in the morning.'

STOW BARDOLPH

An extraordinary collection of memorials to the Hare family demand attention in Holy Trinity church, just off the A10 Downham Market-King's Lynn road. To see the most startling of them all, go to the mahogany case that looks like a wardrobe in the north-west corner, open the half door – and meet the woman at the heart of a bizarre legend.

A face appears behind a window, and there's a grotesquely lifelike wax effigy of Sarah Hare, clad in grubby bodice and scarlet hood, peering out between the tattered curtains. The story goes that she ignored the conventions of the Sabbath back in 1744 and decided to do some sewing. She pricked her finger with a pin and died of blood poisoning at the age of 18. Before she passed away, Sarah ordered that her memory should be kept alive by this life-size model. . .

In fact, she was at least 50 when she died, and that statistic must throw doubts over the rest of the Stow Bardolph legend. Even so, her haunting look defies you to take serious issue with it – or at least until you leave the Hare family mausoleum.

SWAFFHAM

The sign standing proudly at the entrance to Swaffham Market depicts the story of John Chapman, the pedlar reputed to have found a great treasure as the result of a dream. The sign was made in 1929 and given to the town by local craftsman Harry Carter, one of many fine examples of his handiwork in the county. His cousin, Howard Carter, who uncovered the tomb of the Egyptian boy king Tutankhamun, grew up in Swaffham and has been dubbed 'the second pedlar of Swaffham' who discovered even greater treasure. Carter Close, a cluster of new houses on the southern fringes of the town, is a singularly unspectacular memorial to the man responsible for one of the most sensational archaeological finds of all time.

Fate has conspired to make him one of the most famous unsung men of note in Norfolk history. Virtually unrecognised by an ungrateful nation during his lifetime, he remains sadly ignored to this day. Both his parents were born in Swaffham and Howard clearly held the place in considerable affection. It was during those early years in the town that he developed his artistic talent and interest in Ancient Egypt under the patronage of Lord Amherst, a wealthy businessman based at nearby Didlington Hall. Carter was a solitary and difficult man whose background and education may have left him ill-prepared for the deluge of publicity that followed his amazing find in 1922.

Even so, he was a man of great dedication and talent whose contribution to our knowledge of Ancient Egypt deserves far more praise. He was never honoured by his country or the big institutions that benefited from the discovery of Tutankhamun's tomb. He spent his final years in great pain, writing, drawing and lecturing. He died at his London home in 1939 and was buried at Putney.

He got an honorary degree from America and an award from the King and Queen of Belgium. Two exhibitions, the first staged in 1989 to mark the 50th anniversary of Carter's death, represented an attempt by Swaffham Museum to rectify such shabby neglect. Supported by the British Museum, both proved hugely successful – but those who claim to know the true worth of Carter's work want a lasting memorial in the county where he grew up. See also Didlington entry.

SWARDESTON

Nurse Edith Cavell was shot by the Germans for helping Allied soldiers escape during the First World War. 'She died like a heroine,' said the British chaplain who visited her shortly before the execution. That bravery is recalled constantly in the village where she was born and where her father was vicar for nearly half a century.

Edith was born in 1865 in Swardeston in a low, red-brick Georgian farmhouse still known as Cavell House. Her father Frederick had moved to Swardeston, four miles south-west of Norwich, from the neighbouring parish of East Carleton where he had been curate. Edith loved to pick wild flowers on Swardeston Common, still a haven of 40 acres today. Shortly after her birth, Frederick decided to build at his own expense a vicarage next to St Mary's church. The costly Victorian building almost ruined him. Curiously, Swardeston today boasts no less than five vicarages!

Edith began her working life as a governess, including a spell with the Gurney family at Keswick New Hall in the adjacent village, but switched to nursing after being inspired by a hospital she saw on a holiday in Austria and Bavaria. She trained and worked in London before going to Brussels to set up a school for nurses. This became a Red Cross hospital when war broke out. Edith was back in Norfolk staying at her cottage at West Runton on the coast when the grim news came. She went on to play her fearless part in an underground lifeline for Allied soldiers. This led to her ultimate fate. The Germans carried out the execution just a day after her conviction. There was a great outcry and the recruitment rate doubled in the two months after her death. America came into the war, and the Kaiser ordered that in future no woman was to be shot without his personal consent.

Edith Cavell's remains were returned to England in May 1919 for the impressive ceremony at Westminster Abbey attended by Queen Alexandra. The coffin was taken by train to Norfolk and laid to rest outside Norwich Cathedral at Lifes Green. Every year, on or close to October 12th, the date of her execution, a flower festival is held at Swardeston. A corner of St Mary's church has been put aside for her portrait seated with her dogs Don and Jack and a portion of a plain wooden cross returned from Brussels. There are many memorials in the village to the Cavell family, including the village sign which bears Edith's likeness and Frederick Cavell's fine gravestone lying beside the path from St Mary's church to the vicarage he built.

SYDERSTONE

Some of Norfolk's rarest and shyest inhabitants have colonised a corner of this village six miles north-west of Fakenham.

Syderstone's common, 60 acres of heathland, was purchased by the Norfolk Naturalists' Trust in 1978 because of its immense importance to natural history. It is a Site of Special Scientific Interest with large areas of heather, gorse and broom – and internationally famous because of those unusual residents. Star of nature's show is the natterjack toad. It has a yellow stripe down the middle of its back, so it is hardly surprising that this creature runs rather than crawls like other toads. It hides in underground burrows during the day and only comes out at night.

Syderstone is reckoned to have the largest inland breeding colony of natterjacks in Britain. The males have very loud voices in the mating season, so most folk in the village will have heard them even if they haven't seen them. When it comes to breeding the natterjack prefers shallow pools. This often poses a problem because such areas may dry out in summer before the natterjack tadpoles are fully grown.

Norfolk Conservation Corps volunteers have been seen at Syderstone on numerous occasions carrying out tasks for the benefit of the common's wildlife, the natterjack in particular. They have cleared a large amount of encroaching scrub to conserve the other plant life and done considerable work on deepening ponds since they became threatened for the usual reason – water abstraction taking place in the neighbourhood.

TERRINGTON ST CLEMENT

Covering an area of 17 square miles at the base of the Wash, and with a population of over 4,000, Terrington St Clement hardly qualifies for a 'village' label. Old maps reveal small clusters of houses around the church and a number of outlying hamlets centred on the old greens and droveways.

Of the original houses that remain, there are in the middle of the village a few rows of charming old cottages, some former tradesmen's workshops and one or two former shops and pubs, all surrounded now by newer houses and stores.

Lovell's Hall, built in 1543 by William Lovell, Lord of the Manor of Bardolf, one of two principal manors in Terrington, is the oldest dwelling, but Terrington Court is often voted the largest and grandest of old houses in the Marshland village.

Originally known as Hamond Lodge, it was built by Navy captain and Ipswich MP Sir Andrew Snape Hamond in 1810, replacing an earlier house on the site. Constructed in the Georgian style, it remains unchanged, including the remarkable detached pedimented doorway.

The property had several owners around 1900 before becoming a Church of England Temperance Society Home for Inebriate Women. To ensure the lady guests did not disappear for the odd half at the local pub, the boundary walls were topped up with broken glass. Hamond Lodge was bought by Colonel Arthur Hume in 1925 for under £3,000. The name changed to Terrington Court, the jagged glass was removed from the wall and for decades the house became the centre of village life. The listed Grade II house is close to Emosgate Farm in Popes Lane.

THETFORD

The old line about a 'prophet without honour' springs to mind as soon as Thomas Paine is ushered forward to take a bow. No political writer made a more immediate impact on his own era than the man from Thetford. But he had to wait a long time for proper recognition after dying in poverty in New York in 1809.

It was 1945 before he was elected to the American Hall of Fame to stand with George Washington and Paul Revere. Before a statue of Paine was erected in Thetford in 1964 there had only been a bronze plaque paid for by American airmen stationed near the town during the last war. The statue was sculpted by Sir Charles Wheeler, at one time President of the Royal Academy. Paine has a quill pen in his right hand and in his left a copy of *Rights of Man*, written in defence of the French Revolution and making him the spokesman for English radicalism against the oppressive traditions of the 18th century. It sold 200,000 copies and caused Paine to be tried for seditious libel and his effigy to be hanged, shot and burned.

The political dispute over the erection of the statue led to the founding of the Thomas Paine Society, of which former Labour leader Michael Foot became president. While the 200th

Thomas Paine's statue in his home town of Thetford.

anniversary of Paine's birth had been marked by little more than a dinner in the Guildhall in London, the Society saw to it that the 250th anniversary in 1987 was widely acclaimed.

Paine's father, a Quaker, kept a shop in Thetford as a maker of women's corsets, surely the most unlikely parent for a political firebrand. He also ran a small farm and made enough money to send his son to the local grammar school from the age of six until he was 14. The school recently opened a library dedicated to the life and work of one of the county's most undervalued figures.

THOMPSON

One of the Breckland villages affected by the military take-over of the last war, Thompson is in two parts and apparently on the way to nowhere.

Its western parish boundary is part of the ancient Peddars Way. In 1942 the army mapped out the Battle Area right up to Peddars Way, so cutting off Thompson's access to Thetford. The present main thoroughfare to Thetford forms a big curve round the Battle Area. If you are a stranger, taking notice of one of three signposts saying 'Thompson', you will soon find yourself back on the road you just left.

This geographical curiosity apart, Thompson, four miles south of Watton, also reveals some highly unusual features on its nature reserve. Thompson Common, consisting of a mix of grassland, scrub and woodland, contains a number of pingos – shallow ponds formed towards the end of the last Ice Age. They are home to a variety of creatures and plants and look like soaked lunar craters. Many are hidden beneath thick vegetation and trees.

A pingo would have started life as a frozen mound, the ice having pushed up the soil as it solidified and expanded. In melting, the top of the hump tumbled to the edge of the mound, thus creating a crater which filled with water. At the western end of the reserve lies Thompson Watering, a large shallow lake used by wintering waterfowl and waders on passage. Its reed fringe is home to breeding sedge and reed warblers and reed bunting.

A nature trail is open at all times, accessible from the car park in Butters Hall Lane and the Norfolk County Council car park at the old Stow Bedon railway station.

THORNHAM

Locals have been known to boast that there is no land between here and the North Pole. On the coast road a few miles from Hunstanton, Thornham knows a chilly wind when it feels one tearing across the marshes. That hasn't stemmed the growing tide of retired folk and weekend residents moving in, along with facilities for holidaymakers. The tourist trade has taken over from maritime and farming interests as the village's chief concern. Perhaps the pointers were there as early as 1863 when the Prince of Wales (Edward VII) bought Sandringham, the area became fashionable and the railway reached Hunstanton.

A century ago, Thornham was busy forging an unlikely reputation – in ironworks set up by the Lady of the Manor! Mrs Ames Lyde, who lived at The Cottage all her life and not at The Hall, was a woman of great character and drive. Her grand community project began in 1887 when the village population was 550 and parishioners wanted something to do in the evenings. By 1894 orders for lamps, inn signs, gates, railings, balconies, hinges, firescreens and weather vanes had increased sufficiently for two men to be employed permanently. Soon seven forges were installed on the site where the village garage now stands. By 1899 there were five smiths, two bench hands and four apprentices as well as up to two dozen people employed full-time. What was the Oak House, formerly an inn, became the offices and showrooms.

The venture received a big boost when the Prince and Princess of Wales paid a call to inspect garden gates they had ordered for Sandringham and two foliated lamps and a bracket for Shernborne church. Orders now multiplied, coming in from as far away as India and Australia while London architects submitted their drawings to be executed in the Norfolk workshops. Customers included the Countess of Warwick, the Countess of Leicester, Lady Battersea and the Rothschild family. Eighteen pretty hanging lamps were made for Brancaster church. Three gates were made for the Royal Pavilion at the Paris Exhibition of 1900. The Brussels Exhibition of 1911 awarded a gold medal for other gates.

Mrs Ames Lyde travelled throughout Europe for new designs and examples of the best ironwork, but when she died in 1914 and local men went to war her grand project faded. The works were closed down in July 1920 – but some of the glories live on. The original sign showing two men hammering on an anvil is on display with other examples of local handiwork in Thornham Metalcrafts. The King's Head pub sign remains, and in the parish church are the processional cross, candlestick and lectern, the latter paid for by Sunday school pupils 'with their pennies and halfpennies'.

TILNEY ST LAWRENCE

———— A dramatic change in character explains why this village seven miles from King's Lynn pays few if any respects to the memory of John Aylmer. He was born in Tilney St Lawrence in 1521, and became tutor to the ill-fated Lady Jane Grey.

He came early to the notice of Henry Grey, Marquis of Dorset and one of the most powerful nobles in the reign of Edward VI. Having sent Aylmer to Cambridge, the Marquis took him into his household as tutor to his children and to Lady Jane in particular. She thrived on his teaching: 'One of the greatest benefits God gave me is that he sent me so sharp and severe parents and so gentle a schoolmaster... Mr Aylmer teaches me so gently, so pleasantly, and with such fair allurements to learning that I think all the time nothing while I am with him.'

She was doomed to be a pawn in a murderous power game which culminated in her execution in 1554 at 16 years and four months. She spent nine days on the throne. Aylmer took flight to the Continent to escape religious persecution under Mary Tudor. Sunnier days of Elizabeth's reign brought him home and he swiftly moved up the ladder to become Bishop of London.

Then came that remarkable change in personality. All those endearing qualities which had won him the love of his illustrious pupil vanished. In their place came pride, intolerance and intellectual cruelty vented with equal ruthlessness on Roman Catholics and Nonconformists alike. Few mourned his passing in 1594. He was buried in Old St Paul's where the Great Fire of London consumed his tomb.

TRIMINGHAM

——— The parish church is believed to be the only one in England dedicated to the head of St John the Baptist. Trimingham – the name seems deliciously apt for such a legend – was said to be the destination of the head of the Baptist brought from the fortress of Machaerus, beyond Judea, where the great preacher met his fate.

Inspired by this belief, pilgrims once made their way to this small settlement clinging to the north Norfolk coast. The village hall is still called the Pilgrim Shelter, and the comparatively new Poppyland marketing exercise might well have taken a leaf or two out of a much earlier guide to tasteful exploitation. Published in 1854, the *History Gazetteer and Directory of Norfolk* tells us that Trimingham church 'dedicated to St John, was in ancient times visited by pilgrims who came with great offerings to see the head of St John the Baptist which the wily priests pretended they had got.'

A will made shortly before the Reformation mentions the head at Trimingham. Such entries are by no means unusual for that time, referring merely to the numerous representations of the Baptist's head in alabaster, manufactured in Nottingham and Burton-on-Trent. One of these eventually found its way to Trimingham to be associated with some cult or creed.

WATLINGTON

——— A city gent with influence in high places played a colourful role in the chequered history of Watlington railway station. It was opened in the 1870s in this village halfway between Downham Market and King's Lynn. There were lines from Lynn to Wisbech and March and from Lynn to Ely and then on to Liverpool Street in London – part of the original Great Eastern Railway.

Watlington station was given a new name after that city gent boarded the train at Liverpool Street and asked for. . . Watlington station. He duly arrived and discovered he was not in the village of Watlington in Oxfordshire as he had hoped, but in dear old Watlington in Norfolk. Complaints were made. The name was changed to Magdalen Road.

In 1965 came news that the station would be closed to goods traffic. Local growers were up in arms. In the fruit season of the year before they had loaded trays containing 252,820 punnets of strawberries onto the goods trains at Magdalen Road. Some 500 tons of seed potatoes were delivered at the station from Scotland and they also handled 2,500 tons of coal for delivery by local merchants. Petitions and protests were to no avail. Then it was announced in May 1968 that all railway passenger services would end. The station fell victim to Dr Beeching's cruel axe.

Just three years later pressure began to grow in the name of reopening the station as trains were continuing to pass through on their way to Ely and beyond. Magdalen Road Station Pressure Group was formed. Villagers cleaned up the place and restored the Victorian waiting room to its former glory. The official reopening came in May 1975 – and fourteen years later, with hardly a city gent in sight, the old name of Watlington was restored.

WATTON

——— Every community can point to landmarks that ought to have been cherished and saved by a previous generation. In Watton's case, many still point to the cottage hospital and the town pump as examples of facilities that were allowed to slip away.

The sum of £700 was raised by public subscription in 1897 to build a cottage hospital on a site made available by Lord Walsingham on the Thetford road. It was officially opened in July 1899 and named the Victoria Cottage Hospital to mark the Queen's Diamond Jubilee. An operating theatre was added in

1904 and a children's ward three years later at a cost of £200. The building programme was completed in 1933 with a new wing. During its 50 years or so of existence it was used extensively for minor ailments, accidents and maternity cases, and at the annual meeting in March 1947 it was reported that the number of patients for the year before had topped one thousand.

Following the formation of the National Health Service the hospital was closed in February 1950, despite a strong feeling in the town that it should stay open, not only as an asset to local residents but also to help relieve the waiting lists at Norwich hospitals. Members of the East Anglian Regional Hospital Board and the Senior Administrative Medical Officer met local representatives to discuss the hospital's fate, but it was decided it should remain closed. Further efforts to force a change of mind proved fruitless, and the hospital was sold and converted to flats and bungalows, a development now known as Victoria Court. Meanwhile, small hospitals in Norfolk continue to fight to stay open.

The ancient pump had a place of honour in front of the clock tower. Unlike most village pumps that were operated by a long iron handle heavily weighted at the lower end, so being lifted up and down, the Watton pump was unique as it had a circular wheel with a short handle attached to it at an angle of 90 degrees. To obtain water the handle had to be rotated in a circular motion; water came out of a curved spout into a bucket beneath. Any water that overflowed was channelled down to the roadside into a drinking trough for passing cattle on their way to market and for tradesmen's horses. The pump was protected on three sides by sturdy oak posts and iron railings. All were demolished in 1948 despite strong protests. Until the town was converted to the mains supply in the 1930s most residents living near the town centre had to get their water from this source.

WAYLAND WOOD

——— Traditionally the setting for the legend of the Babes in the Wood, this ancient jewel a mile from Watton was mentioned in the Domesday Book and mediaeval boundary banks are still visible. Almost certainly one of the few remnants of the

Wildwood that once covered much of lowland Britain, plants and animals flourishing here provide a direct link with those in the prehistoric forest.

The underwood has been managed in the traditional way as coppice with oak standards, and consists mainly of hazel and bird cherry. Particularly beautiful in early summer, with a profusion of bluebells, primrose, early purple orchid and yellow archangel in flower, the wood is the only Norfolk site where the yellow star of Bethlehem can be found. Its flowers can be seen in March. Wayland Wood is open to visitors at all times.

WELLS-NEXT-THE-SEA

—— What is the link between this little port on the north Norfolk coast and the most famous mutiny in our maritime history? The answer is John Fryer, born in Wells in 1754 and buried in the local churchyard of St Nicholas. He was Master of the *Bounty*, joining the ship in 1787 and at first enjoying good relations with Captain William Bligh. Indeed, Bligh wrote that he was 'a very good man and gives every satisfaction.'

But only a few weeks later he was to promote Master's Mate Fletcher Christian over Fryer's head into the position of acting Lieutenant. Bligh had made an enemy of the man from Wells and it showed in several ways. Fryer was asked to countersign some official documents, but at first refused to do so unless Bligh guaranteed him a good letter of recommendation come the end of the voyage. This was next door to mutiny. Fryer changed his mind when Bligh assembled the crew and read out the Articles of War. Fryer was arrested by the mutineers along with his captain. Together with 17 other men the two were sent down into the ship's boat. The subsequent voyage, an epic feat lasting 43 days, created more tension between Fryer and Bligh. Their relationship reached rock bottom at Timor as they communicated with each other only in writing.

The antipathy continued after they arrived back in England. Bligh refused a request for a character reference for Fryer. In his turn, Fryer aided Edward Christian, Fletcher's brother, in that man's efforts to blacken Bligh's character and save his brother's.

Fryer died in 1817 and is buried in his home town. William Bligh died in that same year. He was 63 as well.

WENDLING

Honeypot Wood, a mile north of this bypassed village near East Dereham, played an important role in the last war. The small ancient woodland formed part of the base for the USAAF's 392nd Bomb Group. Bunkers and concrete rides built for bomb storage now create additional habitats. The rides also enable easy access by wheelchair users to this delightful reserve, owned by the Norfolk Naturalists' Trust since 1987 and open to visitors at all times.

American airmen moved into Wendling in August 1943, using B24 Liberators for combat missions. By the time they had left at the end of May 1945, they had lost 127 aircraft missing in action and another 57 due to operational causes. Nearly 750 airmen died. Many who walk in Honeypot Wood these days and see the small brick buildings and concrete roads think not only of the superb wildlife in this Site of Special Scientific Interest but also of the young Americans who flew out but did not return.

As they speed along the Dereham bypass, most motorists are oblivious to the fact they are passing over the site of the former railway station at Wendling. It was opened as part of the King's Lynn-Dereham line in 1848. The line closed in September 1968, another victim of Dr Beeching's infamous purge.

The road from Wendling village to neighbouring Longham was carried across the railway on an arched bridge to the east of the platform, while Wendling parish church was embowered in trees to the north of the station. The main station buildings at Wendling were in the Tudor-Gothic style incorporating domestic accommodation for the station master and his family.

Eastwards from Wendling, the railway line passed the site of Wendling Abbey, a Premonstratensian house belonging to the White Canons. The abbey was abolished at the Reformation, and apart from a few lumps and indentations in the surrounding field, no visible signs of the mediaeval religious establishment remained. Now, the little railway station is just a memory, although one or two enthusiasts reckon at certain times after dark you can spot oil lamps resting in Great Eastern style lanterns, one of them bolted to the front of the signal cabin. . .

WEST BRADENHAM

——— Henry Rider Haggard, who wrote his way to fame with 50 books including the epic adventure *King Solomon's Mines*, always looked back on his childhood at West Bradenham Hall with great affection. This Georgian mansion stands on some of the highest land in Norfolk a few miles from East Dereham.

When Rider Haggard lived here as a lad in the 1860s he looked out across wooded parklands that sloped away to West Bradenham church and beyond to the river Wissey. The estate, a modest 400 acres, contained a number of farmsteads including Wood Farm, where Henry was born. Returning early from a holiday abroad with another baby on the way, William and Ella Haggard found the hall still occupied by tenants and so retired to the farmhouse.

On the death of his father in 1892, Henry's older brother inherited the estate which he struggled to manage until, by the end of the First World War, failing health and mounting debts forced him to sell up. The hall had been the family home for nearly 150 years and Henry dearly wanted to extend those Haggard links, but together with his Ditchingham property it would have proved too great a burden and so he accepted his brother's decision.

Returning to Bradenham in 1918, Henry wrote in his diary: 'It is odd at the end of life coming back to houses at which one has spent its beginnings, for then such become one vast and living memory. Every bit of furniture, every picture on the walls, every stone and tree bring forgotten scenes before the eye or find tongues and talk.'

Haggard's childhood home also became the setting for L.P. Hartley's novel *The Go-Between*. He stayed at Bradenham Hall in the summer of 1909 as a guest of his schoolfriend Moxey, whose parents had rented the hall from Rider Haggard's brother. It was over 40 years later when Hartley used it as the backcloth for *The*

West Bradenham Hall, where Henry Rider Haggard spent his childhood. It was also the setting for a famous novel.

Go-Between (1954), regarded by many as his best novel and, partly as a result of Joseph Losey's 1970 film version, his best-known work.

Hartley's sister recalled how he first got the idea for the novel and the theme of love destroyed by impossible class barriers from a diary he had discovered at Bradenham belonging to one of the young ladies there.

Even natives who claim to know most corners of their patch need occasional reminders that there are two Derehams in Norfolk. That growing town in the middle of the county has been known to assume a superior stance, almost to the point of dismissing altogether a little cousin way out west four miles from Downham Market. East Dereham has its merits and roll of honour from history. Even so, it has never produced a character to match Hubert Walter, one of the great mediaeval administrators.

Born in West Dereham, he attained the highest honours of Church and State. It was customary in mediaeval times for boys from a good family to leave home at an early age to be brought up in the household of a noble. As a page the boy was under the sort of discipline and training necessary to prepare him to become a squire and to be knighted. To this end, young Hubert joined the family of Radulph de Glanvyle, Lord Chancellor of England. The lad from Norfolk later entered the Church and it was while he was Dean of York that his thoughts returned to his childhood home, where he bought land and founded a monastery. At the Abbey Farm in West Dereham it is still possible to trace remains of that monastery.

Hubert Walter became Archbishop of Canterbury under Richard I and went with him to the Holy Land on one of his Crusades. When the Duke of Austria took Richard prisoner and got the Emperor of Germany to demand 150,000 marks as ransom, Archbishop Walter hastened back as fast as ship and horse could carry him to raise the money. Richard showed his gratitude by making him not only Lord Chief Justice of England but also Lord High Chancellor and Governor of all his realm.

Walter outlived Richard by five years, and even managed to keep some measure of control over his dastardly successor King John. With determination, knowledge and a deft touch Walter developed the system of strong centralised government devised by Henry II. Hubert Walter died in 1205.

Thomas Tusser, the literary farmer who wrote *Five Hundred Pointes of Good Husbandrie*, came to live at Abbey Farm in West Dereham in the 16th century and put some of those points into practice.

WEST HARLING

Breckland was ablaze with autumn colours, nature's last big production of the year, either side of the bustling A11 trunk road. Conditions were perfect for a trip to West Harling. Easier said than done.

Not a signpost in sight. I sought enlightenment in East Harling, the 'big brother' village, more like a small town, nearby. We arrived in Bridgham, another pretty little parish, where a cheerful postman called Peter tried to put us on the right track. He found us flummoxed in the forest half an hour later and felt it best to lead the way. It was well worth the trouble.

Just a handful of houses among the trees, with a handsome church standing back, a wire fence separating it from grazing sheep in the meadows. The regular ripple-like pattern of dark conifers sharpening the simple lines of the tower. A lonely, ancient and intoxicating place.

An important Iron Age site, the area used to be the park of West Harling Hall, built in 1725 and demolished in 1931. Three generations of Cresseners were rectors here for a span of 134 years from 1596, Henry serving for the last 60 of them. For nearly 7,000 Sundays parishioners heard a Cressener in the pulpit. Reluctance to leave this blessed plot was underlined by another long-service record, Richard Deane serving as curate and rector for 57 years through the Napoleonic Wars. Oldest memorial in the church is a brass portrait of another priest, rector in 1470, rejoicing in what must be the most gloriously appropriate name for a leader of the flock – take a bow Ralph Fuloflove.

We stored these little nuggets away, took the advised track through the trees and bumped back into what was bound to be a rather mundane mainstream of Norfolk life. Breckland is full of wonderful secrets. If you want a good chance of discovering them, first find a friendly postman.

WEST RUNTON

This seaside village between Cromer and Sheringham on the north Norfolk coast provided an extra attraction for locals and visitors alike in recent years – the West Runton Elephant. It lay buried unceremoniously for between 600,000 and 700,000 years under thousands of tonnes of rock in a cliff face lashed by wind and sea. The body remained hidden until the storms of December 1990. The first bones were unearthed, and that was the start of the battle to protect and conserve what is said to be the biggest, most complete and best preserved elephant skeleton of its kind ever found.

The project to rescue the elephant bones from the cliff, to clean them up and prepare them for a long future of exhibitions, research and displays began in earnest. Nigel Larkin, the palaeontological conservator in charge of the operation, said the care, patience and attention to detail meant the West Runton Elephant had the best chance of 'survival' possible.

Staff from Norwich and Cromer museums, along with volunteers, launched their rescue in January 1992. They found ribs, jaw, backbone and part of a leg. In 1995 the major excavation work to recover the rest of the skeleton was carried out by the Norfolk Archaeological Unit.

You can see some of the bones and find out more about the background to their discovery by visiting the Castle Museum in Norwich, where a whole modern gallery is devoted mainly to the elephant and includes a life-size hardboard cut-out to show how big it would have been when it was alive – twice the size of one of today's elephants.

WHISSONSETT

This ancient settlement five miles south of Fakenham encircles the parish church of St Mary and hangs on defiantly to rural charms surrendered in so many other places of comparable size. The village sign unveiled in the summer of 1985 provides a useful potted history as well as a proud tribute to the village's most famous sons, the Seagrim brothers, Derek and Hugh. Their father, Charles, was rector of this parish together with neighbouring Horningtoft from 1909 to 1920 and the boys grew up in the village. They are the only two brothers to win the country's top two awards for bravery.

Lieutenant Colonel Derek Seagrim took command of the 7th

Heroic brothers on Whissonsett village sign.

Battalion Green Howards for the Western Desert Campaign in the last war. During the offensive at the Mareth Line he accounted for 20 of the enemy, totally disregarding his own safety and setting an outstanding example to his own men. However, he died of his wounds and in May 1943 the posthumous award of the Victoria Cross was announced. His mother, Mrs Amelia Seagrim, went to Buckingham Palace to receive the decoration from King George VI.

Three years later Mrs Seagrim made history when she returned to the Palace to receive another posthumous award. This time it was the George Cross awarded to Major Hugh Seagrim in recognition of his work and self-sacrifice in Burma. He joined the Indian Army in 1930, and during his leave went on expeditions to the Himalayas where he grew to love the hills and the people. When the Burma Army was reorganised he joined the 19th Hydrabad Regiment as the men who comprised the unit were hill people like his beloved Karens with whom he spent much of his life in Burma. He was chosen to go to the Karen Hills to raise and lead the guerrilla forces and his work was recognised by an MBE in 1942 and the DSO in 1943. It was to save the Karen people from further brutal persecution by the Japanese that he finally surrendered in 1944. He was executed by the Japanese after enduring long periods of solitary confinement.

The village sign, based on the Saxon cross, also depicts a windmill, of which there were two (long gone), the spring well (still going in the lower part of the village), a set of stocks (happily confined to folklore) and an apple, recognising fruit farming as a long-established local industry.

WIGHTON

World-famous sculptor Henry Moore fashioned strong links with this attractive village near Wells on the Norfolk coast during the early years of his illustrious career.

In 1922 his family had moved from Castleford in Yorkshire because of his father's failing health. Henry Moore's sister Mary took over the village school at Wighton. Within a month of arrival, Moore's father died and was buried in the local churchyard. Mary ran the school for three years and during that time Henry, a student at the Royal College of Art, was an enthusiastic holiday visitor.

He used to work on blocks of stone in the schoolhouse yard. This part of Norfolk had a lasting effect on Moore's work. It was here that he began to collect the chunks of flint which abound along the edges of lanes and fields. Their twisted shapes were prototypes for future works of art. He also visited his sister Betty, whose husband taught at Mulbarton, near Norwich, and his brother Raymond, a headmaster at Stoke Ferry in the west of the county.

Even so, Wighton remained his real Norfolk love. In the summer of 1925 Henry wrote to a student friend that if he had the money he would make for 'a country district in England, somewhere like Wighton or Walsingham, and stay there until I'd found and wedded one of those richly-formed, big-limbed, fresh-faced, full-bodied country wenches, built for breeding; honest, simple-minded, practical, common-sensed, healthily-sexed lasses that I've seen about here'. A glowing testimonial of sorts, and here was the inspiration for an army of reclining figures.

A gale blew down the tower of All Saints' church at Wighton in 1965. Thanks to the generosity of Leeds Richardson, a Canadian whose ancestors came from the village, the tower was rebuilt and dedicated in 1976.

 ## WINFARTHING

——— The Good Sword of Winfarthing was a cut above the rest when it came to getting rid of unwanted husbands.

It all began when a thief claimed sanctuary in the village church. On departing he left his sword behind to become the object of 'vow makings, crouchings and kissinges' by folk from far and near. Some came to this parish a few miles from Diss because the sword was thought to help in finding lost goods, particularly stolen or strayed horses. But it was when a wife set a candle before the sword, Sunday in and Sunday out, that a husband had good reason to feel alarmed.

It could be the signal that she wanted to be rid of her lord and master because Winfarthing's wonderful sword was believed to have the power to shorten a man's life. To encourage the help of the sword's powers to finish off a marriage, a wife had to burn a candle before it every Sunday for a year. There is no accurate record of how many anxious husbands saw fit to check on the household candle consumption. A stained glass window in the church commemorates the sword's legendary powers.

A poignant inscription on the pulpit tells of Samuel Bourne, priest here for 13 years. He died in 1865 'giving his life for his people in a fearless act of duty.' He died of smallpox caught while visiting a villager, who recovered and lived for another 60 years to see this tribute to his hero.

 WINTERTON

At daybreak one morning in the autumn of 1921, Winterton Lighthouse went out for the last time, so bringing to an end more than three centuries of sea lights displayed from what was once a remote and notorious part of the Norfolk coast near Great Yarmouth.

On no fewer than four occasions during that time, the Trinity Brethren had established lights here, and as many times again had relinquished them, twice under duress and twice of their own accord. By the First World War, more than 400 yards of valley and dune separated Winterton Lighthouse from the sea. The floating lights out to sea had become so numerous and efficient, and the channel into Yarmouth Roads so well buoyed, that the presence of a lighthouse at Winterton was no longer necessary. So in 1921 it was decided to close the station down, along with its counterpart at Hunstanton which had also outlived its usefulness.

In January 1922, the former lighthouse, shorn of its lantern and gutted of its equipment, was sold by auction. Between then and the outbreak of the Second World War the premises were used as a seaside residence, but in 1939 the site was commandeered by the military authorities, who added a brickwork lookout above the level of the gallery. Apart from this, the end of the war found the tower substantially unchanged and still bearing traces of the overall red coat which had once distinguished it from its striped neighbour at Happisburgh. It then reverted to a private residence, a role it had for the next 20 years. Finally, in 1965, the former lighthouse again came on the market and was bought by the proprietors of the adjoining holiday hotel of which it now forms a part.

When Daniel Defoe, creator of *Robinson Crusoe*, first visited Winterton in 1722, he found a village built almost entirely out of shipwreck and the whole stretch of coast littered with the remains of ships, their carcasses picked clean by local wreckers. He found there were four Winterton Lighthouses: 'The dangers of this place being thus considered it is no wonder that upon this shore beyond Yarmouth there are no less than four lighthouses kept flaming every night besides the lights at Caister north of the town.'

WOLFERTON

Most of the crowned heads of Europe and five generations of British royalty used Wolferton railway station, which served the Sandringham Estate until 1966. It is now a private house and museum. Standing nearby is the Wolferton signpost, telling a complex but fascinating story of its own.

It was put up by George V in 1912, and on top is a picture of an animal looking rather like a wolf and a man with a hand in the animal's mouth. Fenrir is the creature and Tyr is the man, dressed here in mediaeval costume.

The story comes from the time of ancient gods. Woden, king of the gods, discovered Fenrir hidden in a cave. The gods settled on a policy of appeasement, aiming to make the monster gentle by treating him kindly. But Fenrir grew bigger, more savage, cunning and evil. Then the gods resorted to trickery. They said: 'Come, Fenrir, you are proud of your strength. See if you can snap this chain!' The creature let them fasten it and immediately broke free. They tried a stronger chain, but to no avail.

Woden, increasingly anxious about the fate of the earth-folk, sent to the magicians for an unbreakable chain. When it arrived it seemed no more than a silken twist. Again the gods invited Fenrir to try his strength. He replied: 'I will, if one of you will put his right hand in my mouth.' Eventually, Tyr stepped forward. The creature took his hand between his dreadful fangs and the magic cord was wound around Fenrir. The creature strained his sinews in vain. His bones cracked before the silken thread. He bit through Tyr's wrist. The warrior god's sword hand was gone. But evil was fettered at last and Tyr did not count the cost too great.

Wolferton's village sign tells us how futile it is to appease the big bad wolf of evil. Only the faith that right is stronger than might and self-sacrifice born out of such faith can fetter evil.

WORSTEAD

Large and spacious houses in and around this attractive village in north-east Norfolk give clues to an illustrious past.

Weaving looms, 12 feet high, were used when the trade flourished and each house had its own cellar with wooden beams interlacing the ceiling, where the wool was stored at a cool, even temperature. The crypt of one house with a groined ceiling still survives at the bottom of a derelict stair under the bakehouse in the market square.

Other reminders of the weaving industry can be seen in the splendid church. On its floor are several brasses telling the same story engraved in Latin, such as 'Tom Watt, worsted weaver, died 16th August, 1506.'

Worstead gives its name to a type of cloth, worsted, woven in the village in the Middle Ages. From the Conquest onwards Flemish weavers came to England, but it wasn't until Edward II's reign that their cloth came to be known as worsted. Early in his reign Edward III, married to a Flemish princess, actively encouraged immigration of Flemings to 'exercise their mysteries in the kingdom.'

Attracted by abundant supplies of wool in England, a considerable number of weavers settled in and around Norwich where the landscape resembled their native country and where Norfolk sheep produced the same long staple as they had used in

Flanders. This was made into the cloth called worsted, giving both warmth and strength. Thus was founded the name of a skilful trade which brought not only wealth and prosperity to England for 600 years but also provided a household word throughout the world.

By 1830 the weekly wage was up to 25 shillings. Weaving flourished in Worstead for over 500 years. The last weaver, John Cubitt, died at 91 in 1882. Handloom weavers were forced out of business by the power driven machines of the West Riding of Yorkshire, where both water and coal were readily available.

WRENINGHAM

The village pub on the main road is called the Bird in Hand – and the village sign tells a strange story of locals making the feathers fly.

The legend goes that a 13th-century lady of the manor was an evil witch. A knight failed to kill her because she changed into a wren. She is supposed to return every St Stephen's Day and is hunted by villagers who 'beat the hedges with sticks and carry the dead wren in triumph!' There have been no reports of such unlikely antics in recent years.

The sign, designed and made in the village to mark the Queen's Silver Jubilee in 1977, bears the names of the three parishes united in the early 15th century to form the present Wreningham, eight miles south-west of Norwich. On the reverse are coats of arms of prominent families and lords of manors connected with these parishes – St Mary, St Peter and All Saints.

Wreningham Parva, Little Wreningham or St Mary was held by Ketel the Dane in the Confessor's time but eventually passed into the hands of the Bigods, who were to become the first Earls of Norfolk. Nelonde St Peter has also been called Newland, Nayland and Nailyng, and was united to Little Wreningham in 1406. Wreningham Magna or Great Wreningham was united with the other two in 1416 to form Wreningham All Saints, the parish as it is today.

The sign stands on the site of the old village reading room. Members of the local Home Guard, who decided to keep together after the last war, used the building as a men's club.

WYMONDHAM

There's a strong whiff of history about this town – pronounced Windum – despite traffic congestion in the middle and too much development round the edges. Indeed, Wymondham's past comes alive at the Bridewell, enlarged in 1785 as a model prison and now housing an impressive heritage museum complete with cells and a workhouse bier.

The old Elizabethan prison was described as one of the vilest in the country by prison reformer John Howard, who visited the town in 1779 as part of his nationwide tour. He aimed to do away with the old corrupt system where punishments were handed out quite arbitrarily and institute a new regime responsible for both punishing and reforming. Howard described the Wymondham inmates as 'dirty and fickle objects at work with padlocks on their legs', and the prison area as consisting of a men's room to which were attached three 6ft x 4ft 'closets for nightrooms', a separate room for women and an underground dungeon.

After his criticisms, it was agreed to enlarge the Wymondham Bridewell by adding two new wings to the old building, which was now to be used as accommodation for the jailer and his family. This was the first to be built to John Howard's recommendations and became a prototype for new prisons both here and in America. The Bridewell was closed in 1825 when a new extension to the county jail in Norwich was opened. A few years later the Bridewell reopened as a House of Correction for women. Those women sentenced to hard labour operated a laundry for the county jail.

The prison closed again in 1878 and part of the Bridewell became a police station. This remained until 1963 when it moved to its present premises nearby. When women prisoners were moved to Norwich, space became available to allow the Courthouse to be created in 1878–9. In time the Courthouse could expand when the police station moved out in 1963. This third main alternative use of the Bridewell as a Courthouse was its main one from 1932 until the court closed in 1992.

When the Bridewell was converted for use as a museum, the opportunity was taken to carry out an archaeological excavation of the courtyard. This revealed the foundations of earlier buildings, including a mediaeval undercroft.

Before moving into the Bridewell, Wymondham magistrates held sessions in the halls and manor houses belonging to its local dispensers of justice, and later, on the third Tuesday of the month, at the King's Head, one of Wymondham's main coaching inns on the market place. It was demolished in the 1960s and Woolworth's store now stands on the site.

YAXHAM

—— Most Norfolk communities have a bloodcurdling yarn or two to take down from the shelves for a fresh airing, especially for the benefit of newcomers or strangers. These tales are embellished over the years and it can be difficult separating fact from fiction. A few defy analysis of any sort.

Yaxham, with a definite identity of its own despite being so close to the fast-growing town of East Dereham, provides a strong double bill of murder most foul. Cut Throat Lane tells the ancient tale of how a young woman of easy virtue met her untimely end. Clifton's Field is said to be the scene of another murder in the village, with the murderer hung in chains from a gibbet in Yaxham for the edification of the inhabitants. This dark chapter was given added authenticity by an article in the *Dereham and Fakenham Times* in October 1932, recalling how a man called Clifton dropped in at the bar-parlour of the inn which stood in Church Lane. That inn was called the Great A, distinguished as it was by its queer gables, the ends of which were shaped like large capital As. The property still stands. . .

'While Clifton was sipping his ale, a hearty, loud-voiced farmer came in, clearly pleased with his day's business. A few drinks later he was even more pleased with himself and became very generous with his money, revealing to all that he had a large amount in his pockets. Realising the possiblity of rewards for himself, Clifton befriended the farmer and pretended to be interested in all he said. The farmer enjoyed Clifton's company and they left the inn as lifelong friends.'

The story goes that Clifton took him a quiet way along a path which used to lead from the church towards the mill on the Mattishall road. Clifton murdered his man in a field and stole his money. That piece of land is still called Clifton's Field. . .

Clifton was caught, found guilty and hanged outside the county jail in Norwich. Then his body was taken to Yaxham and hung in chains for all to see and to serve as a warning to other would-be criminals. The newspaper report went on: 'They were obeying a dark law of savage times which said that by exposing the murderer's body near the scene of the crime, the spirit of the victim was avenged.'

Years later, Clifton's Field was ploughed up 'and Clifton's skull came to light. The older generation of the village passed that skull round from hand to hand, and now that skull can be found in Norwich Castle Museum.'

That 1932 article has never been refuted in any vehement way, and the murder stories continue in lively circulation.

INDEX